Strange Land

Wycliffe Studies in Gospel, Church, and Culture

GENERAL EDITOR: THOMAS P. POWER

The series entitled Wycliffe College Studies in Gospel, Church, and Culture is intended to present topical subject matter in an accessible form and seeks to appeal to a broad audience. Typically titles in the series derive from sermons given by the faculty of Wycliffe College, Toronto, in its Founders' Chapel. The current volume on Ezekiel is the eighth in the series.

OTHER TITLES IN THE SERIES

Confronting the Idols of Our Age.
ED. THOMAS P. POWER

The Lord's Prayer.
ED. KAREN STILLER

Come, Let Us Sing to the Lord: Songs of Scripture.
ED. KATHERINE KENNEDY STEINER

Redemption and Relationship: Meditations on Exodus.
ED. ANDREW C. WITT

The Word is Near You: Seeds of the Reformation.
ED. PETER M. B. ROBINSON

Behold, I am Coming Soon: Meditations on the Apocalypse of John.
ED. MARI LEESMENT

Strange Land

*Meditations on the Psalms
in a time of Pandemic*

EDITED BY
Caris Kim

WIPF *&* STOCK · Eugene, Oregon

STRANGE LAND
Meditations on the Psalms in a time of Pandemic

Wipf & Stock
An Imprint of Wipf and Stock Publishers
199 W. 8th Ave., Suite 3
Eugene, OR 97401

www.wipfandstock.com

PAPERBACK ISBN: 978-1-6667-1688-7
HARDCOVER ISBN: 978-1-6667-1689-4
EBOOK ISBN: 978-1-6667-1690-0

08/11/21

Contents

List of Contributors | vii
Introduction | ix
  —Caris Kim

1 The Master of Mercy | 1
  —Ephraim Radner

2 Seek His Presence Continually | 9
  —Joseph Mangina

3 A Plunge into the Deep Waters of
   Being Humans Who Worship God | 17
  —Ann Jervis

4 A Joint Venture with Re-creation | 23
  —Annette Brownlee

5 Making a Joyful Noise to the Lord | 30
  —Alan Hayes

6 What to Sing in a Pandemic | 37
  —Stephen Andrews

7 Let All That Is within Me Praise the Lord | 42
  —Peter Robinson

8 And David Says, "Sing!" | 48
      —CATHERINE SIDER-HAMILTON

9 Restoration | 55
      —THOMAS POWER

10 Hope and Prayer amid Displacement | 62
      —GLEN TAYLOR

11 The Malnourishment of Separation | 71
      —DAVID KUPP

12 Remembering and Passing on the
     Unabridged Story of God | 80
      —MARION TAYLOR

   Bibliography | 89

List of Contributors

Stephen Andrews, Principal and Helliwell Professor of Biblical Interpretation, Wycliffe College

Annette Brownlee, Professor of Pastoral Theology, Wycliffe College

Alan Hayes, Professor of Church History, Wycliffe College

Ann Jervis, Professor of New Testament, Wycliffe College

David Kupp, Professor of Pastoral Theology, Wycliffe College

Joseph Mangina, Professor of Systematic Theology, Wycliffe College

Thomas Power, Adjunct Professor of Church History, Wycliffe College

Ephraim Radner, Professor of Historical Theology, Wycliffe College

Peter Robinson, Professor of Proclamation, Worship and Ministry, Wycliffe College

Catherine Sider-Hamilton, Professor of New Testament, Wycliffe College

Glen Taylor, Emeritus Professor of Old Testament, Wycliffe College

Marion Taylor, Professor of Old Testament, Wycliffe College

Introduction

CARIS KIM

"WAKE UP, ALICE DEAR!" In the final chapter of Lewis Carroll's *Alice's Adventures in Wonderland*, Alice's sister wakes her up while she is screaming and trying to fend off an animate pack of cards that are following the Queen's order to kill her.[1] Finally, Alice realizes that her strange adventures were merely a dream. After this awakening, the story ends with two sisters talking about Alice's dream and drinking tea. For over a year we have been suffering from the COVID pandemic, which seems like a bad dream that someone would wake us from, as Alice's sister does.

One more thought that, for me, arises from Alice's story concerns the *Sitz im Leben*, the "setting in life" of the book and its author. In the case of this classic book, we know exactly which year it was published in, when and where the story was originally written, and the real person the author modeled Alice after. We even have her photograph and his illustrations of her. We know the author's real name, his pen name, his major at the University of Oxford, and his political, religious, and personal

1. Carroll, *Alice's Adventures*, 187.

orientations. His edited private diaries and medical history can also be easily obtained.[2]

Contrastingly, in the case of the Psalms, which were written several thousand years ago, scholars acknowledge that it is not possible to reconstruct fully the historical backgrounds of the text or to determine the identity of all its writers or editors. Scholars who study Lewis Carroll complain about the large gaps in the information about him, but the type and quantity of information they already have is what biblical scholars dream about. I can only imagine what it would be like to know all of the *Sitz im Leben* of the psalmists. I await the time when we shall see the Lord—and each other too—face to face and know fully, instead of seeing "a reflection as in a mirror" and knowing only in part, as we do now (1 Cor 13:12 NIV).

However, even without this information, the authors featured in this volume help us understand the Psalms and connect us to the psalmists in our own *Sitz im Leben*. They show that we can get closer to the texts without further searching for the psalmists' contexts. In this volume, the contributors help us engage with and apply the Psalms in the following ways. First, they illuminate and proclaim who God is according to the text; that is to say, they inform us of how the psalmists portray God. For example, Ephraim Radner presents God as our "master," which is not a preferred word in our modern context but occurs in Psalm 123 and many other places in the Bible. Radner effaces the negative connotations of the word by associating it with mercy, which can be understood as "unexpected grace" that only a "master casts upon a subject gratuitously." God is the master of masters and the good master.

2. Woolf, *Mystery of Lewis Carroll*, 1–5.

Even though God is our master, Joseph Mangina argues that God is the one who invites human beings into personal communion with him. Mangina observes that the psalmist presents God as the named God, so he can be sought continually in our whole life. He argues that this is the way we love God—seeking him and wanting to spend time in his presence. Mangina also points out that by retelling God's mighty acts performed on behalf of Israel, the psalmist encourages Israel to proclaim his works among the nations because his deliverance is not limited to Israel.

Second, knowing God eventually leads to worshiping God, so the contributors direct our attention to the worship of God in the Psalms—the ways in which the psalmists worship God or the ways in which they expect readers to worship him. Ann Jervis focuses on the fact that the Psalms encourage us to worship God, and she describes acts of worship as the "most not-self-focused of activities." In a time when it is easy for us to focus selfishly on ourselves as we stay away from others, she warns us that if we do not extol God, we are lost "in the downward spiral of our complaining, fear, and self-focus." She concludes with the observation that our narcissism breaks as we see the Lord's holiness. In reflecting on Psalm 114, Annette Brownlee recognizes that the psalmist extends the range of worshippers to the whole created world, including hills, mountains, waters, rock, and the earth. They witness and react to God's actions and participate in his redemption of Israel. Unlike human beings, they respond obediently to God's saving actions on behalf of Israel. Therefore, Brownlee affirms that worship is "a joint vocation" or "a co-operative venture between humans, their landscapes, and God." Alan Hayes declares that the command of the psalmist to "make a joyful noise unto the Lord" in Psalm 100 is not only for the ancient Israelites, but applies across generations and even beyond the boundaries of the human race to all aspects of creation.

Hayes recognizes as well that taking joy in the Lord when we feel locked in joylessness is the greatest challenge of our Christian discipleship, but he notes that it comforts us to consider the fact that the psalmist knows exactly the same challenge. Stephen Andrews asks whether the recitation of a victory psalm would be poor timing for us now. Should we postpone it until the virus gets under control? He says no, because "in declaring the greatness of our God, even in the direst of circumstances, we join with those who have gone before us in piercing the darkness with praise, where the shafts of light that stream in from heaven become the avenues of God's justice." Catherine Sider-Hamilton gives us an example of someone who sang a praise song in the midst of affliction and loneliness that he was experiencing for the sake of God's kingdom. It is David, who wrote, "The Lord will save those whose spirits are crushed" in Psalm 34:18. This lyric is repeated by Jesus in Matthew 5:5: "Blessed are the poor in spirit, for theirs is the kingdom of heaven" (NRSV). Sider-Hamilton keenly points out that David knew that Jesus would protect all of David's bones because Jesus made a pledge with his own bones (Ps 34:20), and she argues that this is the reason why we sing with David today. Through an analysis of Psalm 82, a lament over God's abandonment and absence, Thomas Power adds that our "waiting, pleading, and crying out" to God is legitimate and is part of the answer to our questions. The reason is that salvation depends only on God and that our pleading is a privilege in his grace.

Third, the contributors assess the current pandemic as they interpret the Psalms. Peter Robinson observes our modified worship during the pandemic and appropriately points out, "Livestreamed worship carries something of the echo of our worship together, and we can hope that it will sharpen the hunger that soon we may be able truly to gather to enter into the presence of God, to lift up our souls to him." Robinson thinks that this waiting for corporate worship is also a part of Psalm 25, as seen in verse 5, which says, "For you I wait all the day long" (ESV). He suggests that we continue to speak the Psalms together while we cannot sing together, because "the psalms give voice to the character and nature of the Holy One and also give voice to our hopes and fears."

Glen Taylor engages with our *Sitz im Leben* by answering a question in light of Ps 106. The question is one that many Christians have thought of during the COVID pandemic: is this the consequence of someone's sin? Taylor notes that in Psalm 106:6 the psalmist confesses his sin, and Taylor makes the following statement twice: "A time like this ought naturally to lead us to self-examination, not to blame ourselves or anyone else specifically, but to consider what sins we might have committed (not that caused the pandemic, but in general) and to name, confess, and repent of them." He also advises us to prepare for the pandemic of coming divine judgment, to pray for the end of the social isolation that the pandemic has necessitated, and to remember the "primacy and privilege of praise in corporate worship."

Drawing on his reading of Psalm 85, David Kupp considers the possibility of permanent scar tissue in our post-pandemic life setting. He makes an inquiry into the failures of the psalmist's life setting, arguing that the collapse that Israelite society faced was entire, including the "socio-economic, ecological, and spiritual" spheres. The "malnourishment" seen in Psalm 85 is the result of "our hunger for divine presence" and the extremely limited relationships between "community members, neighbors, colleagues, and friends." It concerns Kupp that this collapse can bring long-term consequences that establish a pattern of chronic malnutrition in every sphere of society. However, since this psalm ends with the expectation of God's restoration, Kupp encourages us to seek the Spirit's wisdom in the hopes that it will renourish our community.

Lastly, Marion Taylor recommends making the psalm the *mashal* of our mouth for the sake of our descendants. The word *mashal* in this psalm refers to mysterious enigmas from earlier times that the psalmist's ancestors remembered and passed on (78:2). Taylor points out that throughout the Old Testament we can see the repeated failures of the Israelites to respond to God in obedience. Most of the time it is because of their amnesia with respect to God's mighty works for them and his commandments. In Ps 78, the psalmist chooses not to hide the story of Israel's failure, in the hope that their children would remember "both God's great acts of salvation and his commandments" and know that "their lives are to be characterized by obedience, reverence, and covenant faithfulness." Taylor remarks that we are called to remember and teach "a thorough and unabridged account of the story of God" to our descendants.

Over the past year, we have seen that the fear of death caused by the pandemic has stopped the world. In this book, each contributor not only tries to narrow the gap between this ancient book and the contemporary reader, but also encourages us to endure and enjoy our lives in our life settings in this "strange land." The authors recognize our weaknesses and remind us about the saving power of Jesus's death for us. They try to make the "difficulties and impediments," as one contributor says, "*constitutive* of the saving power of Jesus Christ" that transforms our hearts.

1

The Master of Mercy

Ephraim Radner

Here is the text of Ps 123 in the KJV:

> Unto thee lift I up mine eyes, O thou that dwellest in the heavens.
>
> Behold, as the eyes of servants look unto the hand of their masters, and as the eyes of a maiden unto the hand of her mistress; so our eyes wait upon the Lord our God, until that he have mercy upon us.
>
> Have mercy upon us, O Lord, have mercy upon us: for we are exceedingly filled with contempt.
>
> Our soul is exceedingly filled with the scorning of those that are at ease, and with the contempt of the proud.

We are perhaps inured to the way the language of slavery suffuses the Bible. The language of slavery in the Bible, which is ubiquitous, tracks the horrors of this unending human practice. And after the shackles are shaken and broken, assaulted and thrown off, the language remains, still resonates, as if it is something one can never get away from. Nor, perhaps, should we. Certainly, we cannot do so with Psalm 123. For where else shall we find mercy, the mercy we so desperately need not only in a time like ours but in lives like ours? Where else but from a master, not simply a friend, but a sovereign *master* who binds the beasts and deceivers of this world in chains (Rev 20:20) and takes "captivity captive" (Ps 68:18; Eph 4:8)?[1]

So, we come to the psalm. "Unto thee lift I up mine eyes, O thou that dwellest in the heavens" (Ps 123:1). Such is the place of God, the psalmist tells us over and over: high in heaven. "He that sitteth in the heavens shall laugh: the LORD shall [scorn them]" (Ps 2:4); "The LORD's throne is in heaven: his eyes behold, his eyelids try, the children of men" (Ps 11:4); "But our God is in the heavens: he hath done whatsoever he hath pleased" (Ps 115:3). Power, judgment, derision, doing whatever he wants! God in the heavens is literally above all *this*, this mess that covers the earth, because of a kind of power that puts him beyond the realm of any other being's control and responsibility: he can laugh; he can hate (Ps 5:5); he can bring into being; he can destroy (Isa 45:7); he can do "whatsoever he hath pleased." He is the absolute master of all things.

We tend to think of a master as a tyrant or capricious despot. In the master-slave relationship, no doubt that is, alas, a common character. Furthermore, the master-slave relationship is exactly what is in mind here in Psalm 123. God is master in the sense of a slave master, and the psalmist is a slave. The KJV of verse 2 uses "servant," but in fact the Hebrew "'*ebed*", which corresponds to the Greek *doulos*, refers to a human victim who is *in the power* of another—captive, bound, bonded, chattel.

---

1. Unless otherwise noted, all Scripture quotations in this chapter are from the KJV.

Precisely here our modern presuppositions are challenged. In a way, the psalm does open up a terrible window into human history: slavery, until about 160 years ago, was assumed to be a common human ordering of life, a common and virtually universal reality. This truth is something we forget.[2] When the Normans invaded England in the mid-eleventh century, about 10 percent of the entire population of southern England were slaves. The slave trade out of what later became the city of Bristol was already thriving in the year 1066, as thousands were being taken, bought, sold, and transported to Ireland and then to North Africa. This system had been established centuries before, as we vaguely remember from the story of the English slave boy known later as Patrick or from the story of the British captives sold in Rome's marketplace whom Pope Gregory I called "not Angles, but Angels," afterward sending missionaries to Britain, as Bede tells us.[3] Much later, of course, Bristol was to become the center of another, vaster economy of slavery, spanning western African and the Americas. We still suffer from its reach and horror. But the point is that slavery is not new. It is estimated that in St. Paul's time, literally a quarter to a third of the population in Italy were slaves, and fully a fifth—20 percent—of people in the larger Mediterranean world were being bought and sold as slaves. We can keep going back in history, of course: Solomon enslaved his own people, as was predicted by Samuel (1 Sam 8:10–18; 1 Kgs 12:3–14), and David himself was surrounded by slaves who did his bidding and abetted his sin. Shall we descend to Egypt or reach out to Babylon and Assyria? Most people knew what a slave was;

2. Rodriguez, *The Historical Encyclopedia of World Slavery;* Heuman and Bumard (eds.), *The Routledge History of Slavery.*

3. Bede, *A History of the English Church and People,* bk.1, chs. 23–25.

they saw them, owned them, were themselves such people, or knew the possibility was ever lurking—as still it is, we sorrow to say. Human slavery was a thread woven through the fabric of every human society from Greece to China.

And what of God? He was their master. He *is* their master. He is ours. And because slavery was a pervasive part of human society, "mastery," the role of master and mistress, was far more varied than the singular monster of our modern imagination. There were good masters, and society and human life itself depended on their existence. St. Paul will call sin and death a "master," and they are indeed the worst of all possible overseers, stalking us as "lords" of our existence (Rom 6:9). But God, too, is "master," as in verse 2 of our psalm, wherein we are placed in the role of the slave. We look to God "as the eyes of slaves look to the hand of their masters" and as slave girls look to their mistresses. The word "mistress" here—which is rare in the Bible—is used to describe Sarah in relation to the slave Hagar (Gen 16) and Naaman's wife in relation to a captive Israelite maid (2 Kgs 5:3). But the human master here is *"adon"* in Hebrew, which, as we know, is also the name for the Lord of heaven and earth, though in the plural, *Adonai*. "The hills melted like wax at the presence of the Lord [*Adonai*, the Master, the master of masters], at the presence of the Lord [the master] of the whole earth" (Ps 97:5). We are used to thinking of God as a king, but kings were masters.

"So our eyes wait upon the Lord [the Master] our God, until that he have mercy upon us" (v. 2). Masters, too, can have mercy. Indeed, only a master can give mercy of the kind any human being might finally yearn for, mercy that can pierce all the layers of dominion that cover the world and its history from start to finish and finally seem to crush us. As I said, St. Paul understands human existence as a great field in which competing masters seek to subjugate us. These masters are sin and its deputies and barons—greed, human power, idolatry, death itself—and all of them are absolutely *merciless*, without pity. Nothing has changed in that regard throughout human history: however much we plead for money's tender touch, or power's gentle caress, or idolatry's loose embrace, or, finally, death's forgetful glance—Isaiah 28:15 shockingly speaks of our "covenant with death," implying a deluded human notion that we can reach a diplomatic compromise with its unrelenting grip— these masters all "sweep through" in an overwhelming torrent, as Isaiah says (28:19 NIV), mercilessly.

"Have mercy upon us, O Lord [the Lord of Lords, Master of masters], have mercy upon us" (v. 3). We can identify each one of these cruel lords in our lives and in people around us—the disloyal friend or lover, the grasping and unforgiving colleague. We see them also in the avaricious claims of the necessities of earthly existence, including our bodies, each of which, bit by bit, grinds us down. Is there no master greater than these, a master greater than all these masters, a master of mercy itself? The word used in this psalm that is translated as "mercy" might be derived from a word referring to just that look of pity or favor, that unexpected grace, that only a master casts upon a subject gratuitously, an "inclination," literally, of the eyes, a moment of notice, a sense that, at least here, there is space given within the infinite scope of infinite power for just this person, for just you, for me—and think of our time—for us. "Have mercy on us, Lord," we say, peeking at some small tremor of the hand in heaven that might give rise to hope. "As the eyes of slaves look to the hand of their master . . ." (Ps 123:2 NIV).

Only a master can have such mercy, and only a master above all masters can have such mercy as overcomes the world's unrelenting tyrannies, its oppressions of contempt and pride and scorn, and all the assaults of the petty but awful despots in our lives and societies—count them up if you will: anxiety, injustice, illness, drugs, sorrow, prejudice, disgust and despair—of which we have had more than enough (Ps 123:3–4). He who is in heaven laughs them to scorn (Ps 2:4). The scorn of this Master, the scorner of the scorners who holds in contempt all the contemptuous masters of the earth, is our mercy.

Have mercy on us, Lord!

We know the stories: the Lord walks by us and a woman of Canaan, the slave land, the "slave of slaves (RSV)," as Noah says of Canaan (Gen 9:25), and she cries out, "Have mercy on me, O [Master], thou son of David; my daughter [lies oppressed by] a devil" (Matt 15:22). And I have cried this prayer too, repeatedly. As the Lord continues on his way, and as we lie beside the road, beset and blinded—each of us knows by what—we cry out, "Thou son of David, have mercy on me!" (Luke 18:39). Jesus the Lord and Master, have mercy.

Jewish interpreters have traditionally viewed Psalm 123 as a psalm of exile—words spoken by Israel, scattered and captive, awaiting *Mashiach*, the Messiah. This understanding is a helpful orientation for Christian interpreters too. Nonetheless, as Christians we are not still waiting; we say or sing Psalm 123—"Have mercy upon us, O LORD! (v. 3)—as those who also speak, who have already gone on, "by degrees," to the next psalm, 124. For here, in Psalm 124, we are firmly set in a present that has built on a fulfilled past:

> If it had not been the Lord [the Master] who was
> on our side, now may Israel say; . . .
>
> Then they had swallowed us up quick, when
> their wrath was kindled against us: . . .
>
> [But] our soul is escaped as a bird out of the
> snare of the fowlers: . . .
>
> Our help is in the name of the Lord, who
> made heaven and earth. (Ps 124:1, 3, 7–8)

That is Psalm 124. Jewish interpretation is hardly
wrong, in one sense: we still stand as slaves beset by the
scornful, capricious, and evil masters of the world. Yet, we
know—we *know*—that the eyes of the slave, our eyes, *are*
noted, they *are* understood, their glances *are* taken into the
heavens themselves and brought back to earth. As Philippians 2:5–11 tells us, although Jesus was God, he became
a slave even to the point of death and is therefore "highly
exalted" (v. 9) above all names and above all masters. He
is the great Master Lord whose infinite power made him a
slave like us.

So, we dare *not* become inured to the language of
slavery in the Scriptures, both its sorrow and its pity; for
if we do, we lose the glimpse of what God has done, of the
strangeness but also the astonishing power of his mercy. It
is powerful because God's mercy thus goes to the heart of
who we are and where we are. It is astonishing because it
marks, not caprice, but the whole person of God himself. It
is strange, ever so strange, because it turns the scorn for the
universe, cosmic scorn, divine scorn, into a form of compassion the likes of which enter our fretful and tremulous
hopes and fill them to the brim. We have had more than
enough of the world's, of our leaders', of our neighbors', of
COVID's, of life's contempt. Yet, here, the Master of masters comes among us. It is *he* who speaks first in this psalm,
by the way: "Unto Thee lift *I* up mine eyes" (v. 1). The "I" is

the Son of God. It is "I" first, and the "our" and "us" follow. We follow in this psalm, and we follow in human life. For Jesus "lifted up his eyes to heaven, and said, Father, the hour is come; glorify thy Son, that thy Son also may glorify thee" (John 17:1). "Unto thee lift I up mine eyes"; and the slave becomes a child, and the Master becomes the Father we have waited for.

Scripture: Psalm 123

Questions

1. In what way does the language of slavery in this psalm fit with other biblical texts regarding the relationship of human beings to God?

2. Does calling God "master" demean him or us?

3. How might the exercise of divine power escape the charge of divine tyranny?

4. What does it mean to call Jesus a "slave"?

5. Is "mercy" a simple synonym for "love"? And if not, what might the distinctions between these two concepts imply with respect to God's relationship to us?

2

Seek His Presence Continually

Joseph Mangina

THERE IS SOMETHING JUST a bit odd about preaching on a psalm. To preach is to expound the word, the word being God's speech, or address, to us. But the Psalms are—almost by definition, one could say—our speech to God. They contain our prayer, and praise, and complaint, and lament, and cry for help. How can our word to God be God's word to us? There is a good argument that the Psalms are not to be preached on but simply to be *used* in church, spoken or said as part of the liturgy. Perhaps we might say that a psalm should not *mean* but *be*. But as a matter of fact, the Psalms are Holy Scripture, and the entire fabric of Scripture is the divine word. Therefore, it cannot be amiss to preach on the Psalms, even if there is something strange about it. So, my task here is to unpack the divine word in the human word. Just what is the psalmist on about in Psalm 105 (which, I must admit, I had never paid much attention to before this preaching assignment)?

Well, what he is on about is praise and thanksgiving. "O give thanks to the LORD, call on his name, / make known his deeds among the peoples. / Sing to him, sing praises to him; / tell of all his wonderful works" (vv. 1–2).[1] The psalmist thereby reminds us of the fundamental human situation before God: the acknowledgment that he is the giver and we are the receivers, that God is the worthy recipient of human praise, both because of who he is and because of what he has done, namely, performed "wonderful works." To praise God is to know that God is God and we are not, and that is a very good thing. There is a scene in the movie *Monty Python and the Holy Grail* in which a rather grumpy-looking God the Father—it is one of those amazing Terry Gilliam cutouts—appears in the sky to King Arthur and his men, at which point they all fall to the ground in terror. The LORD is not pleased: "Don't grovel," he says. "One thing I can't stand is people groveling . . . It's like those miserable Psalms; they're so depressing."[2] But even when the Psalms are about sin and repentance, they are not "groveling," much less depressing, but rather razor-like efforts to tell the truth about human life in the presence of God. And this psalm does not even strike that penitential note. Psalm 105 is a jubilant hymn, a song, an expression of thanks to the Lord for his mighty deeds for Israel and before the nations.

Notice that the psalmist summons Israel to call on the *Name* of the Lord and to glory in that Name. All this is found within just the first three verses. The fact that the Lord has a Name—the four Hebrew letters *yod*, *he*, *waw*, and *he*, rendered in English as YHWH—is of incalculable importance, not only for Israel's but for the church's faith.[3]

1. Unless otherwise noted, all Scripture quotations in this chapter are from the NRSV.

2. "Monty Python & The Holy Grail—A Blessing from The Lord," 1:07.

3. In most English editions of the Bible, the divine Name is not spelled out but is represented by the word "Lord," written in capital

You might think that the higher you rise on the ladder of divinity, the less important particular names become, so that when you arrive at the very top, you just have some nameless Transcendence. But this is not what the Bible tells us. The God of Holy Scripture is the named God, the God who wants human beings to call on him by Name. God is a person—*the* Person—and invites us to personal communion with him. There are, of course, other biblical names for God besides the Tetragrammaton. In the Old Testament, we have "Elohim," "Adonai," "El Shaddai," and "El Elyon." In the New Testament, we have "Father," "Jesus," "Lord," and the baptismal formula "the name of the Father and of the Son and of the Holy Spirit" (Matt 28:19). But all of these names ultimately go back to the one Name revealed to Moses at the burning bush, a Name so holy we do not even speak it but honor it by our reverent silence.

Now, because the LORD has a Name, he may be sought. "Seek the LORD and his strength; / seek his presence continually" (Ps 105:4). This is the one little bit of Ps 105 I already knew, though I could not have told you where it was from. I knew it because it is used by St. Augustine in book 1 of his famous treatise *On the Trinity*.[4] The LORD wants us to seek him, to find him, to cling to him, and not to let go. As the woman says in the Song of Songs: "By night on my bed I sought him whom my soul loveth" (3:1 KJV). And he wants us to do this *continually*; this seeking will color our whole life. It will be a seeking for one we already know and love but strive to know and love more deeply. As Anglicans and Protestants, we do a great deal of talking about God's love for us, and rightly so; it is the heart of the gospel. Yet, we could do a much better

---

letters. This custom reflects ancient Jewish and Christian practice.

4. Augustine, *On the Trinity* 1.3.5.

job of talking about our love for God, as commanded by the Torah and by Jesus himself. If we do not love God—if we do not seek God, want to spend time in God's presence, "hang" with God, you might say—then it is not clear why we should even bother with being Christian. In Jesus, God has made time for us and summons us to spend time with him, to "seek his face continually." We catch a hint of this theme in Philippians 1:21–26, where Paul says that his deepest wish is to be with Christ—right now, in the heavenly places where Christ is—but is willing to delay that joy for the sake of his churches.

Whom does the psalmist summon to seek the Lord's presence? Israel, naturally. His song is spoken to "the offspring of [God's] servant Abraham, / children of Jacob, his chosen ones," as we are told in verse 6. The Psalms are the songs of Israel, temple music. Indeed, it is a fascinating thing that the first fifteen verses of Psalm 105 are quoted in 1 Chronicles 16:8–22, where we see David using them to celebrate the coming of the ark of the covenant to Jerusalem after its exile among the Philistines. This psalm shows Israel *being* Israel, dancing and capering before the LORD like King David.

But one cannot talk for very long about Israel without stumbling sooner or later across the nations. "O give thanks to the LORD, call on his name, / make known his deeds *among the peoples*" (v. 1, emphasis added), writes our poet. The LORD's wonders and miracles are not the business of Israel only, but also of the nations, the '*ammim*, the people who worship strange gods and are, in fact, Israel's enemies. We see this in a big way in the central portion of our psalm, verses 7–36, which are omitted in the Revised Common Lectionary, no doubt for reasons of length. In essence, this part of the psalm retells the story of

Israel's going down into Egypt, her oppression there, and her deliverance by God's mighty acts. There is a double point being made: on the one hand, the psalm shows God's care for his people through acts of power, even in the direst circumstances of suffering and oppression; on the other hand, the psalm highlights God's *demonstration* of that power before the eyes of the astonished nations. The nations are a part of the LORD's story with Israel, whether they like it or not—indeed, whether they know it or not. Echoing Exodus, the psalmist reminds us, in verse 38, that once the plagues started, the Egyptians could not be rid of the Israelites soon enough. But though Egypt and the other nations are Israel's natural enemies, they, too, belong to the LORD. So, whatever the future redemption of Israel will look like, it will have to involve, somehow, a future for these "others" whom the LORD has made and who form part of his mysterious design for his creation.

This brings us back to St. Augustine. Augustine, of course, is reading this psalm in Latin. He does not know much Hebrew. But he does know a bit of Greek. He notices that in verse 1, where the psalmist writes, "Make known his deeds among the peoples," the Greek version of the Old Testament uses the verb *apanggeilate*, which means "to declare or announce." The verb is related to the noun *euanngelion*, the New Testament word for news or glad tidings that we often translate as "gospel." Augustine therefore translates the sentence as "Preach the gospel of his works among the gentiles." Augustine then asks, "To whom is this addressed, if not unto the Evangelists in prophecy?"[5] Augustine is surely right about this. On the one hand, the psalmist's words are spoken to Israel, the offspring of Abraham and Jacob. *They*, the special recipients of God's

5. Augustine, *Exposition on the Book of Psalms,* 1025.

blessing and favor, are to declare his works among the nations. Israel's vocation to do this will never end, for hers is an everlasting covenant. But the Lord's mightiest work of all will be the incarnation, life, death, and resurrection of Jesus Messiah. Therefore, these words are also spoken to the Evangelists, to Matthew, Mark, Luke, and John, who will declare the miracle of God's coming to us in Christ. They are also, for that matter, spoken to us, who are ourselves gospel bearers and apostles of the good news. It is our glad task to summon the gentiles—along with Israel—to praise and thank the LORD and to seek his presence in the face of Jesus Christ.

Of course, Psalm 105 does not try to tell the whole story of the exodus or of Israel's wilderness wanderings. It does not say anything about grumbling or rebellion or the death of the sons of Korah for their disobedience (Num 16:1–35). There is a place for talking about these hard things, but this is not it. Rather, the psalmist simply wants to create a space for pure doxology, pure thanksgiving, and praise. This is a song about the sheer *generosity* of God, and it is a summons to give thanks in the face of God's goodness to his people:

> He spread a cloud for a covering,
>> and fire to give light by night.
> They asked, and he brought quail,
>> and gave them bread from heaven in abundance.
> He opened the rock, and water gushed out;
>> it flowed through the desert like a river.
> For he remembered his holy promise,
>> and Abraham, his servant. (vv. 39–42 ESV)

As I have lived through these months of the pandemic, this strange COVID-tide in which we find ourselves, I have discovered in myself an enormous capacity for grumbling. I do not like wearing a mask—certainly not preaching in a mask! I do not like having to spend two weeks in self-isolation after traveling outside the country. I do not much like Zoom church or, now that we are back in our building, having to sanitize my hands before and after receiving the Eucharist, where we receive bread only and no wine. Complain, complain, complain, or in the expressive language of Yiddish, *kvetch, kvetch, kvetch.* My capacity for complaining gives me something to pray about. There is much that is different about the church in COVID-tide, and it can leave me—as perhaps it leaves you—feeling dispirited and discouraged.

But here, my friends, is the good news. God is good. He protects us in our sojourn among the nations. He still rules the nations, even though they, in their foolishness and pride, still rebel against him. He is still the giver of every good and perfect gift, in COVID-tide and in every tide. And that means our basic vocation as Christians has not changed: we are still a people of thanksgiving, a eucharistic people, who have been showered with bread from heaven beyond all our deserving. Christ is that bread from heaven, the one in whose face we may seek the LORD continually, the gift that keeps on giving and that summons forth endless praise, whether in Israel or the *ekklesia*[6] or the nations. So, "give thanks to the LORD, call on his name, / make known his deeds among the peoples."

Scripture: Psalm 105

---

6. This is the usual Greek word for "church" or "Christian assembly" in the New Testament.

Questions

1. Read Psalm 105 aloud, from beginning to end. What nuances, if any, emerge that you might have missed simply by reading it silently?

2. This chapter spoke of the importance of the biblical God being a named God. Read Exodus 3:1–15. Does God give Moses an answer to his question about the Name or not? How would you interpret this passage?

3. The Bible frequently speaks of human beings seeking God, longing to be in his presence (see, e.g., Ps 27:4). At the same time, God is described as the one who seeks the lost (Ezek 34:16, Luke 19:10). What is the significance of these two kinds of seeking?

4. This chapter suggested that we often do a better job of talking about God's love for us than about our love for God. Do you agree? What would be the signs of a life devoted to loving God?

3

A Plunge into the Deep Waters of Being Humans Who Worship God

ANN JERVIS

ONE OF THE BASIC tensions we all struggle with is whether it should be about us or about someone else. This struggle between self-focus and other focus is there in all our relationships, a struggle between narcissism and altruism or, better put, the struggle to find the way of love. This struggle is there in our family relationships—how much, and when, should we focus on ourselves , and how much, and when, should we honor and give space for the lives of our spouse, our parents, our siblings, our children, our other relations? This struggle is there in our work relationships: how much, and when, should we protect ourselves from the demands of others, and how much, and when, should we give generously so that others have fewer demands? It is there in our societal relations. How much, and when, should I give money to a street person, and how and when should our church demand rights for what we believe is central to the gospel? And this tension between focus on ourselves and focus on others exists in our relationship with God.

We see this in the Psalms. In each of the five books of the psalter, there are both laments and hymns. There are psalms that give vent to the longings and disappointments and fears that a person or the community feels, psalms that say to God, "Look at me, at us," that declare that I or we matter and expect more; and there are psalms that focus not on the self but God, looking outward to ponder the majestic wonder of the Lord.

The Psalms as a whole ask us to contemplate whether our life is about us or God. Perhaps it would be better to say that the Psalms offer us a plunge into the deep waters of being humans who worship God. The 150 biblical psalms are profoundly human and faith-filled prayer poems that describe the search for that fine balance between acknowledging our needs and acknowledging God's holy power. They are an entry into the medium of faithful struggling between, on the one hand, our egos and the egos of our community and, on the other hand, our desire to be turned away from ourselves and toward God.

Psalm 99 is on one side of that struggle: it gives voice to, and even enables, an intense and transformative turn to the contemplation and adoration of the Lord God. I want to delve into this beautiful psalm but to do so reminding us that it is part of the mixture of lament and praise that make up the psalter. Psalm 99 is contextualized by the honest toil of all the voices of the psalter reaching out and even praising God in the midst of very, very difficult circumstances. This psalm, like the other psalms of worship, is not situated in a glorious, stress-free beach vacation. In the case of Psalm 99, which is found in book 4 of the psalter, the historical situation reflected is most likely the struggle of Jewish exiles in Babylon trying to make sense of their lives.

Psalm 99 is clearly not a lament. It is a hymn of praise to God. There are no complaints, no requests; the psalm is all about God, and it praises the God who reigns. The Lord is King! God's rule is so tremendous that those who see it tremble. The unfathomable vastness and immensity of the greatness of God's rule is illustrated by a glimpse of the Lord seated on a throne. The only response to the high and mighty Lord is quaking and praise. And the praise that the psalmist asks for is the acclamation "Holy is he." Twice the psalm pauses to shout out these words (vv. 3, 5).[1] The psalm ends by instructing the hearers to "extol the LORD our God, / and worship at his holy mountain; for the LORD our God is holy" (v. 9).

Along with this directive to proclaim God's holiness, the psalmist offers other descriptions of the Lord. The Lord is a lover of justice (v. 4); the Lord has deep connections with humans. Moses and Aaron were among his priests. Samuel called on his name (v. 6). The Lord spoke to them and revealed his ways to them (vv. 6–8). The Lord answered them and both forgave and punished them (v. 8).

This psalm looks away from the self—outward toward the Lord. And what the community sees is the holiness of God. The Lord is *qadosh*, holy. Holy is he. There is no more dramatic way to escape the bounds of self-focus than to recognize that the Lord is holy. This recognition pushes us to an outward gaze even more than saying that the Lord is entirely just and powerful and forgiving—other features of God that the psalm underscores. To proclaim "Holy is he" is to proclaim the Lord's otherness. It is to proclaim that the Lord is not an extension of us, that he cannot be fit into our space. When we see the Lord's holiness, it shatters our

1. Unless otherwise noted, all Scripture quotations in this chapter are from the NRSV.

narcissism. We see that God is the Other, the most other that we can possibly fathom. God's holiness is God's otherness, both in his moral sanctity and in his being. God is thoroughly holy in character, so he is pure justice, pure goodness, pure forgiveness, pure judge; God is thoroughly holy in being and is therefore incorruptible and eternal. This psalm guides us to worship, that most un-self-focused of activities. We are to worship the Lord who is not us.

That last thought may sound banal. Of course the Lord is not us. But how often do we forget that? Does our God look like us to us? Do we assume that God cares about, or is even on our side of, the political causes of our time? In the first century AD, Pharisees who were plotting with the Herodians because they were afraid found themselves unable to contain Jesus' influence. They therefore tried to draw Jesus into the debate about paying taxes to Caesar. Jesus, God's Son, would not enter that fray. "Give to Caesar the things that are Caesar's, and to God the things that are God's" (Mark 12:17 CSB). Do we assume that God's ways are our ways? Are we really looking at ourselves when we think we are looking at God? How often do we tremble at the awareness of God's holiness, God's otherness?

And what is lost if we do not extol the Lord our God and tremble at his holiness? We are. We are lost. We are lost in the downward spiral of our complaining and fear and self-focus. For we are not made for self-focus. We are made to gaze on the Lord. Augustine famously put it, "You have made us for yourself, O Lord, and our hearts are restless until they find their rest in you."[2] When the psalmist enjoins us to proclaim that God is holy and extols us to worship God, this is because that is what is best for us.

2. St. Augustine, *Confessions*, 21.

The thing about God's holiness is that it itself is other-focused. God's holiness is not a sanctimonious standing-apartness. God's holiness is not the same as aloofness and remoteness. In fact, it is the opposite. God's holiness is his connection and care and profound love for his world. God's holiness is holiness that does not keep itself unapproachable and remote, as if he were enthroned on the cherubim, saying, "Hey, look at me." God's holiness is with and for us. As Hosea 11:9 puts it, the Lord is "the Holy One in your midst"; as Isaiah 12:6 puts it, "Great in your midst is the Holy One of Israel." As the incarnation of the Lord's Son reveals, God's holiness is his becoming like us so that we could become other than ourselves—or, better put, other than ourselves trapped in only ourselves—and become like the Lord. God is holy, and God is with us and for us. This is his holiness. And unless we get out of ourselves and see this, we are lost in the inward gaze that leads to despair.

This strange and disorienting pandemic moment tempts us, in our isolation, to focus on ourselves. We may be living in close quarters, having to negotiate who does the housework, who does the childcare, who gets some work time or downtime; we may be living alone, having to struggle with too much of ourselves all the time. Psalm 99 is a call to us to look outward, to gaze on the great one whose throne is winged angels, to tremble at the Lord's holiness. It is a call to fall down and worship the Holy One who asks us to look at him looking at us. And it is a call to find, in the light of God's gaze, the way of love.

Scripture: Psalm 99

Questions

1. What are your most un-self-focused of activities?

2. As you have read Psalm 99, have you moved away from your focus on your inner self and proceeded to the holiness of God?

3. Do you have too much time to focus on yourself? How can you gaze outward and look at the Lord's holiness in this pandemic moment?

4

A Joint Venture with Re-creation

Annette Brownlee

THE EIGHT SHORT VERSES of Psalm 114 cover centuries of God's faithfulness to Israel, from slavery in Egypt to their exodus through the Red Sea into the wilderness and, later, through the Jordan to the promised land. But its compactness is surpassed only by its beauty. There is so much that is beautiful to notice. First, its structure is well formed. The eight short verses are divided into four units of two verses, with each verse composed of two parallel lines. Second, the psalmist tells Israel's history in a splendid way: not in covenants or dates but by the reaction of the waters and mountains to God's saving actions. The psalmist's eyes are directed to the trembling of the created world in response to God. Our eyes follow, and we look upon the parted sea through which the house of Jacob flees, the rushing Jordan held back. "The mountains skipped like rams, / the hills like lambs" (v. 4).[1]

---

1. Unless otherwise noted, all Scripture quotations in this chapter are from the NRSV.

What ails you, the psalmist asks the mountains, that you so skip and tremble? Could it be their response to the giving of the law on Mount Sinai? Many think so.

What the psalmist describes is strange for us to think about and hard to know what to do with. First, we find a created world that witnesses and reacts to God's actions in his history with Israel. There are hills and mountains that skip, waters that turn back. Second, we find a created world that does more than witness and respond to God's actions. In verse 8, the psalmist describes a created world that *participates* in God's redemption of Israel. At God's command, hard rock becomes water, flint becomes flowing springs. Rock and stone created by God here co-operate with him in his creation of Israel by obediently responding to his word. As a result, God's people can make it through the all-too-real wilderness.

The psalmist seems to be saying this: the history of Israel, as of the church, is not primarily a human enterprise or even a joint divine and human enterprise. It seems to be a co-operative venture between humans, their landscapes, and God, who is the creator and redeemer of both.

What are we to make of this as followers of Jesus Christ, we who like so many—we are not exempt—must sit before our computer screens because of COVID and mourn its devastation and deaths?

Now, Psalm 114 is certainly not the only place Scripture describes such a joint venture. Once you start looking, it is all over the place. The created world *witnesses to* God's actions and *participates in* them. Remember what happens in Genesis 4, right after God's good creation of the world in Genesis 1–3. The ground God has just made steps in as a witness to human disobedience to God's good ordering of his world. Cain has killed his brother Abel. God says, "Your brother's blood is crying out to me from the ground! And now you are cursed from the ground, which has opened its mouth to receive your brother's blood from your hand" (vv. 10–11). In the book of Deuteronomy alone, three times Moses calls on heaven and earth to witness to the covenant (4:26; 30:19; 31:28). "Assemble before me all the elders of your tribes and all your officials, so that I can speak these words in their hearing and call the heavens and the earth to testify against them." Ezekiel prophesies not only to the people but to land, mountains, forests, soil, and wind (6:2; 7:2; 21:2; 35:2; 36:1). And those who try to silence the crowd of disciples who praise Jesus as he enters Jerusalem? They discover that they have no power to silence the created world's praise of Him. Jesus declares, "I tell you, if these were silent, the very stones would cry out" (Luke 19:40 ESV).

We can say at least this: the land is not just a stage on which the drama of God's relationship with his people is played out. Any disinterest in the created world because of the promised return of Jesus is misplaced. But I think the psalmist nudges us to go further. For whether the created world is praising God, or witnessing to God's mercy or judgment, or participating in either of these things, it is always in *response* to God's word. What is startling about this psalm is this: it is not so much that God speaks to the created world; after all, God speaks it into existence. It is that the created world responds and that the response is always obedient.

If only we could, we would obey God's voice like the rivers and mountains, the rock and flint. And do we not know this? God has come nearer to us than he did at Mount Sinai or the Jordan or in the wilderness when the rock became water. God became our flesh; sent us his Son;

joined us to himself in his body, the church; calls us his brothers and sisters; and gives us his own ministry and Spirit until his return. And yet, unlike the Jordan and the sea and the mountains and the rock, most people are not driven back from their sins, do not tremble at his presence, and are not moved in the paths of obedience.

God tells us as much through the prophet Jeremiah: "I placed the sand as a boundary for the sea, / a perpetual barrier that it cannot pass; / though the waves toss, they cannot prevail, / though they roar, they cannot pass over it. / But this people has a stubborn and rebellious heart; / they have turned aside and gone away" (Jer 5:22–23).

Elsewhere in Scripture, not so much in Psalm 114, which is a psalm of praise, the landscape responds to human disobedience with its own kind of mourning (Jer 2:12–13; 12:7–13; Hos 4:1; Amos 1:2). Its mourning is expressed by drought and desolation. In his first lament, the prophet Jeremiah asks, "How long will the land mourn, / and the grass of every field wither? / For the wickedness of those who live in it / the animals and the birds are swept away, / and because people said, "He is blind to our ways" (12:4).

What we must notice is this: the joint venture between humans, the landscape, and God cuts all three ways. We need the created world's obedient response to God's word for our flourishing. We need the cycle of seasons, and we need rain and snow to water the earth. Likewise, the created world is dependent on our obedience for its flourishing. And both the created world and humanity are dependent on the obedience of Jesus to his Father for its redemption and re-creation.

It is Jesus' obedience to his Father that led him to give up equality with God, to take the form of a servant. His obedience led him to the garden and then the cross. The earth trembled at his death; the skies grew dark. When the women ran to the tomb on Easter Day and found it empty, they did not know it yet, but they were witnessing God's final and decisive word on his created order. In the resurrection of Jesus, God has stood by his creation. God has not let it come to naught. Death will not prevail. Through Christ's resurrection and ascension, God has redeemed the whole thing. Christ's resurrection is a joint venture with re-creation.

So, God tells us, "If any of you could break my covenant with the day and my covenant with the night, so that day and night would not come at their appointed time, *only then* could my covenant with my servant David be broken" (Jer 33:20–21, emphasis added). God's covenant with the night and day stand firm. So does his covenant with his people. Christ joined himself to us, and he frees us so we can take our proper place within the created order. This brings us back to the present, the time of the virus. Throughout Scripture, the earth's mourning is linked to the state of the whole human community—Israel, Judah, all wicked inhabitants of the earth. We do not need Scripture to tell us that the created world is far from impervious to negative effects resulting from human activity. But what global warming alone cannot tell us is what the psalmist tries to point to: it is the obedient response to God that sustains all of creation, the obedience of Jesus to his father, the obedience of the created world to God's word, and our obedience to that same word—the Word made flesh. Obedience, it seems, is also a joint venture.

All this is good news for us, especially in a time when there is global warming and a pandemic, a time when so much has been disrupted and the future seems up for grabs. There is no change to the narrow way that God gives us to live on and to witness on in his world: it remains—and it is perhaps more crucial now than ever—the narrow path of joyful obedience and sacrificial love for those who take on the form and mind of Jesus Christ. In his service, which is service to our neighbor and the created world, is found perfect freedom.

This might seem like small potatoes—magical thinking—in this time: how is it going to stop the fires and droughts, produce and distribute vaccines, and bolster the economies of the many countries that are struggling tremendously? The narrow way of Christ can seem dry, lifeless, and useless. Its difficulties are real.

But these difficulties and impediments are *constitutive* of the saving power of Jesus Christ. The ineffectiveness we perceive in the narrow way of Christ is part of the potency of the promised new life, for this supposed ineffectiveness forces us to submit ourselves to a lifetime of obedient searching in the very narrow way of Christ; otherwise, especially at a time like this, we abandon the path as inauspicious and lifeless. The weakness—its foolishness, as St. Paul describes it (1 Cor 1:18)—forces us to look again rather than look elsewhere.[2]

Let this difficult year be a season of looking again and responding with one another in obedience, looking again and responding with one another and with the created world in obedience.

In our short and beautiful psalm, there is only one verse, verse 7, where we are addressed. It is a command that is not just for us.

> Tremble, O earth, at the presence of the Lord, /
> at the presence of the God of Jacob.

2. Reno, *In the Ruins of the Church*, 114.

God is mentioned for the first time here. All of God's created world is commanded to tremble—that is, to respond in obedience to his saving actions to Israel. It will not surprise you to hear me say that worship, like obedience, is a joint vocation.

We can tremble along with the mountains and rivers, forests and fields. God has promised that he will not break his covenant with the created order or with us, his people. And God cannot and will not be unfaithful to his word.

"Tremble before him, all the earth," 1 Chronicles 16:30 says. "Yea, the world stands firm, never to be moved" (RSV). The earth will not be moved, even in this strange time.[3]

Scripture: Psalm 114

Questions

1. Can you think of any other examples from the Bible in which the created world responds to God obediently?

2. How can we co-operatively join God's redemptive work during this pandemic?

3. I am grateful for Wycliffe graduate Mari Jørstad's excellent doctoral dissertation, which I consulted as background for this meditation. See Jørstad, "Life of the World."

5

Making a Joyful Noise to the Lord

Alan Hayes

"Make a joyful noise unto the Lord!" (Ps 100:1).[1] At first sight, this exhortation seems to come from a very different place than the confession of Psalm 123, which, as Professor Radner tells us in this book, arises from a profound sense of our need for God's mercy. But perhaps they are not so very different. The psalmist very frequently moves between our need for God and our joy in God. Indeed, our need for God and our joy in God are bound together. Recognizing that God, the sovereign of all that is, can give us the mercy that we long for brings us joy. And even when God's mercy seems to elude us, even when God seems eclipsed from our view, we can try to follow the psalmist in remembering the many signs of God's love and faithfulness that have prompted us to sing for joy in the past. These are our warrant for seeking God's mercy.

"Know ye that the Lord he is God," the psalmist says (v. 3). Our falling short of God's goodness is the reason we

1. Unless otherwise noted, all Scripture quotations in this chapter are from the KJV.

recognize our need for God's mercy in Psalm 123. The fact that God is good is the reason we sing for joy in Psalm 100.

In both our need and our joy, words can fail us. Sometimes our need is so great that the Spirit has to intercede for us with "sighs too deep for words" (Rom 8:26 NRSV). There is no speech, just sighs. And sometimes our joy is so great that our most authentic response is simply to make a joyful noise. Again, there is no speech, just joyful noise. In fact, we are not the only ones that the psalmist calls to make a joyful noise. All the lands, all the earth, all creation are to join with us in making a joyful, rapturous, musical, thankful noise.

Yes, it can be hard to sing for joy when our child is sick or someone we love dies or justice is denied or famine strikes or we are abused or we are struck by the misery of so much of the world. To recall our capacity to take joy in the Lord when we are experiencing fear, hurt, and despair is perhaps the greatest challenge of our Christian discipleship. As the Anglican poet George Herbert writes,

> Joy, I did lock thee up: . . .
> And now, me thinks, I am where I began
> > Sev'n yeares ago: . . .
> I did towards Canaan draw; but now I am
> Brought back to the Red sea.[2]

There is no sure remedy for the discouragements to our faith. But over the centuries, many have taken some comfort in the fact that the psalmist knows exactly this same dilemma. Knowing that Psalm 123 and Psalm 100 will each speak to us at different times in our lives and that they are different songs rooted in the same faith and inspired

2. Herbert, "Bunch of Grapes."

by the same God can sometimes, by grace, help us catch a glimpse of a better place.

Psalm 100 has a special place in the worship of Israel. For one thing, it is the great doxology that caps the praises of God the King in the previous seven psalms.[3] One of its partners is Psalm 96, which also invites all the earth, and all creation, to make a joyful noise to the king: "Let the heavens be glad, and let the earth rejoice; / let the sea roar, and all that fills it; / let the field exult, and everything in it! / Then shall all the trees of the forest sing for joy" (vv. 11–12 NRSV). All these psalms of thanksgiving can ground our souls while they raise our hearts. But Psalm 100 is also special because, in the morning prayers of the synagogue, many Jews stand only for this psalm, just as in George Frederic Handel's *Messiah*, Christians will stand only for the "Hallelujah Chorus."[4] A Jewish midrash on Leviticus from the early Common Era affirms that in the future age all songs will be nullified except for this one, just as all sacrifices will be discontinued except for the thanksgiving sacrifice.[5]

This vision of thankful joy as Israel's destiny is grounded in the promise of Psalm 100 that we are God's people, the sheep of God's pasture. Now, I have dealt with sheep in my life. Sheep are not very good at looking after one another, or even themselves. They tend to go astray, and when that happens, the other sheep do not

3. This meditation was originally prepared as a sermon that was preached in the week of the celebration of Christ the King.

4. An interesting discussion of why some Jews stand for Psalm 100 while others do not can be found on Mi Yodeya, a question-and-answer site for Judaism; see "Why Do People Stand."

5. A midrash on a verse in Leviticus says that in the future age all sacrifices will be annulled, except for the thanksgiving sacrifice; in the synagogue, Psalm 100 was substituted for the thanksgiving sacrifice (*Vayikra Rabbah* 9:7).

help. They will probably just keep grazing to satisfy their own needs. Alternatively, they may say to themselves, "I wonder whether that sheep who is wandering off knows something that we don't know," and then they follow and wind up equally astray. Sheep are vulnerable to predators, accidents, poachers, and unknown forces, and they would not last very long without a shepherd, or at least a sheep dog. We, too, like sheep, are a bit dense, inept, self-centered, vulnerable, and liable to go astray. We, too, need a good shepherd. Thankfully, the psalmist says that we have one. The shepherd may not always succeed in protecting us from ourselves, but the good shepherd will always come looking for us. For that assurance we can be profoundly thankful.

Psalm 100 gives another reason for our thankful joy. When so much around us is fake or harsh or bad, "the Lord is good; his mercy is everlasting; and his truth endureth to all generations" (v. 5).

When the psalmist calls Israel to enter God's gates with thanksgiving and God's courts with praise, we can imagine a procession to the temple after which the priests of Israel will make sacrifices. Similarly, our joyful noise is a participation with all the covenant community in a liturgy of praise. But Psalm 100 points us far beyond the boundaries of our religious community. There is that first verse: "Make a joyful noise unto the Lord, *all ye lands.*" We may not think of Judaism as an evangelistic religion that seeks to make converts, but the mission of that little nation of Israel is somehow intimately bonded to God's will for the whole wide world. When God blessed Abraham, God told him, "In you all the families of the earth shall be blessed" (Gen 12:3 NRSV). The prophet Isaiah proclaimed that

God intended Israel to be a light to the world (60:1–3).[6] And since, in Christ, God has made a way for us who are gentiles to enter the covenant, we, too, rise to our divine calling to be instruments in the blessing of all the families of the earth. Our joyful noise is not intended to separate us from the non-Christian world, but to identify with it.

Now, when the psalmist tells us to make a joyful noise, an academic like me is very tempted to respond, "Well, instead of making a joyful noise, I think I will just *analyze* joyful noises." What are the criteria of joyful noises? What are the methods of making them? What are the expectations and outcomes? How can we evaluate the joyfulness of the noise? And to be sure, since some of our noises do indeed arise from the wrong kind of joy and are unpleasant to God, we do need to exercise judgment. But I find that our theological analyses and debates, not just in our seminary classrooms but in our church synods and denominational newspapers and elsewhere, all too often overshadow our joyful noise. So, I invite those who may read this to take time now to turn your hearts and minds and imaginations to the joyful noise that people around the world and across the centuries have lifted to the heavens as they have been inspired by the word of God and as they have experienced God's overflowing love and mercy.[7]

6. This is a theme of Second Isaiah (chs. 40–55) in general.

7. In the original form of this little essay, when it was a sermon, I invited the congregation to enter into the music of Christians around the world: Byzantine chant, the gospel K-Pop of So Hyang, West Indian gospel praise, the music of Christian sitarist Sanjeeb Sircar, the Wallah African drum and dance ministry, the "Laudamus te" section of François Poulenc's *Gloria*, a bagpiper's rendition of "Amazing Grace," and "Glory, Glory: When I Lay My Burden Down," sung by Archbishop Mark Macdonald at an Indigenous gospel jamboree. For reasons of time in a chapel service, I had to excerpt all of these, but I hope that readers will take time to enter into the entirety of whatever

The world is full of human voices singing praise to God. And these are not just the voices of people in the present; they are also the living echoes of voices through the centuries who have praised Jesus Christ since his birth in Bethlehem. How great and loving is our God, who has made the hearts of all the company of saints glad with music with which to sound our joy.

But now imagine those other voices as well, the non-human voices of our brothers and sisters in God's wider creation: the mountains and the hills and the trees of the field that Isaiah says will break forth into singing and clap their hands (Isa 55:12); the sun and moon, the shining stars, the waters above the heavens, the sea monsters, and the fire and snow, all of which praise the Lord (Ps 148); every creature in heaven and on earth and under the earth and in the sea proclaiming blessing and glory to the one who sits on the throne and to the Lamb (Rev 5:13); the beasts and the birds of the heavens and the fish of the sea that teach us God's ways (Job 12:7–10); the trees of the wood that sing out at the presence of the Lord because God comes to judge the earth (1 Chr 16:33). I have begun to look to our Indigenous Christian brothers and sisters to help me enter more deeply into the scriptural vision of a creation that God intends us not to exploit, but to join with, so that I can hear its joyful noise and bring my own joyful noise into closer harmony with it.

Whenever we offer our music to God, we are not alone; we are joining our voices with all of creation to the glory of our good and merciful and caring shepherd. And whenever we make a joyful noise to God, it becomes not just noise but a voice in a great symphony of music offered to the ears of God.

------

selections of the world's "joyful noise" that they choose.

For this privilege of making a joyful noise, this vision of the creation's praise of God, this calling, and this glory, thanks be to God.

Scripture: Psalm 100

Questions

1. As you have lived through the pandemic, what has given you joy in God, and what has made you aware of your need for God's mercy?

2. Have you had periods of joylessness like George Herbert? Have they worried you? What have you done about them?

3. In verse 1 it says, "Make a joyful noise unto the Lord, *all ye lands*!" (KJV, emphasis added). Whom do you think "all ye lands" includes? Does it include you?

6

What to Sing in a Pandemic

STEPHEN ANDREWS

THE PSALMS WERE AMONG the most preached-on texts in the early church and in the period of the Reformation. Why? Our forebears understood better than we, perhaps, just how central a role the psalter played in early Jewish and Christian worship. For there is ample evidence within the collection of the poems themselves that this was the prayer book of communities and of individuals. Indeed, Dietrich Bonhoeffer would go so far as to say that "the Psalter is the prayer book of Jesus Christ."[1] Readers of the Gospels will know that Jesus frequently takes the words of the psalmists on his own lips, and he even chides those on the road to Emmaus for their ignorance of them: "This is what I meant by saying, while I was still with you, that everything written about me in the law of Moses and in the prophets *and psalms* was bound to be fulfilled" (Luke 24:44, emphasis added).

---

1. Bonhoeffer, *Life Together*, 46. See also the entire section "The Secret of the Psalter," pp. 44–50.

So, any attempt at understanding both the mind of Christ and the message of the apostles must resort to the psalter. In fact, Martin Luther once remarked that the psalter

> might well be called a little Bible. In it is comprehended most beautifully and briefly everything that is in the entire Bible . . . In fact, I have a notion that the Holy Spirit wanted to take the trouble himself to compile a short Bible and book of examples of all Christendom or all saints, so that anyone who could not read the whole Bible would here have anyway almost an entire summary of it, comprised in one little book.[2]

That should be enough to make us want to study the Psalms, but it must also be added that while many of the poems arose from particular historical events, they have applicability to the joys and frustrations, the hope and despair, experienced by God's people in every time and place. There are few texts of any sort that can both comprehend and speak into the unusual circumstances we find ourselves in today. Is not Psalm 149:5, for example, an exhortation to the church in the era of COVID, with all of its Zoom services?

Let the faithful rejoice in triumph;
  let them be joyful on their beds.

Let me briefly say a couple of things about this psalm. The first is that it is a doxological psalm. The word "doxology" comes from the Greek word *doxa* (δο΄ξα), meaning "glory." "Let the saints be joyful in glory," exclaims the same psalm (v. 5 KJV; cf. v. 9). "Doxology" is a word that students of Wycliffe College become used to, as it frames the overriding aim of all our theological thinking. The purpose of theology is to change the world. More, however,

2. *Luther's Works*, vol.35 Word and Sacrament, p.254.

needs to be said, for bad theology can change the world for the worse. So, how will we know whether our theology is good? It is good if it ascribes honor, beauty, and grandeur to God and if its transforming purposes are aligned with his purposes in the world.

Psalm 149 offers us a doxological sandwich. At the heart of the poem is a beautiful line describing God's redeeming purposes. Verse 4 reads,

> For the Lord takes pleasure in his people
> and adorns the poor with victory.

There is something both heartwarming and humbling about the affirmation that "the Lord takes pleasure in his people." The idea of God delighting in those whom he has made (v. 2) is not uncommon in the psalter, but the thing to note is that it is never presented as a response to human effort or achievement.[3] Indeed, Psalm 51 explicitly says that the Lord takes "no delight in sacrifice" (v. 16).

Then who enjoys God's pleasure? It is not the kings and nobles, for they will be bound in fetters, says verse 8. Rather, it is the humble. It is the undeserving. It is those who know that they have no claim on God's compassion, who are aware of their unworthiness and who feel keenly their profound need. These are the meek-hearted, the crippled, the ruined. The true sacrifices of God "are a broken spirit" says Psalm 51:17 (KJV).

The Lord "adorns the humble with victory" (v. 4 NRSV). There is comfort in these words, to be sure, especially for students starting a new term and feeling a sense of intimidation in the face of the task they have taken upon

3. Cf. Psalm 147:11: "the Lord takes pleasure in those who fear him" (NRSV). The verb "to take pleasure in" something or someone occurs some thirteen times in the psalter (MT 40:14; 44:4; 49:14; 50:18; 51:18; 62:5; 77:8; 85:2; 102:15; 119:108; 147:10, 11).

themselves. But placed in the larger context of what is going on around us, we might be hard-pressed to imagine ourselves adorned with victory.

Few things in my lifetime have underlined our poverty and inadequacies like the current pandemic. The fracturing of our worship communities; the isolation from our families, friends, and colleagues; the disruption of our habits and routines—these have been deeply unsettling. We all know people who have lost jobs, and we may be among those who have concerns about our own health or the health of loved ones. A great many are worried about the future, about the security of investments, and about the economic viability of governments. One is tempted to ask, then, "Is the recitation of this psalm mistimed?" Should we postpone it until the long season of the virus gives way to the season of reopening?

The answer must be no, for as we have said, this psalm has found a home in the worship of God's faithful, humble people for millennia. The reason is that in a variety of ways, and by means we often do not understand, God's victorious purposes are always being worked out. For the psalmist, God's faithfulness in the past was demonstrated in the transformation of a group of slaves and semi-nomads into a chosen nation. And for us, who were once estranged from God, we are now "no longer strangers and aliens," but "citizens with the saints and also members of the household of God" (Eph 2:19 NRSV). And this redeeming work will continue in every act of doxology until every tongue confesses that Jesus Christ is Lord.

My friends, it may seem inappropriate, impudent, or audacious, but we are bidden everywhere and always, in defiance of the physical and spiritual viruses that would seek to dishonor God and distort his creation, to join in the doxological acclamation, "Praise the Lord!" For in declaring the greatness of our God, even in the direst of circumstances, we join with those who have gone before us in piercing the darkness with praise, where the shafts of light that stream in from heaven become the avenues of God's justice.

Scripture: Psalm 149

Questions

1. The Lord "crowns the lowly with victory" (v. 4). What does victory look like for God's people today? What does it look like in your life?

2. What does it mean for the faithful to "exult in glory" (v. 5 NRSV)? What inspires you to praise God?

3. The Church has sometimes been called "the frozen chosen." What prevents us from being known as a doxological community? How can the church be more doxological?

7

Let All That Is with-
in Me Praise the Lord

Peter Robinson

"To you, O Lord, I lift up my soul" (Ps 25:1).[1]

So begins this hymn of corporate worship. The sim-
plicity makes the line's significance easy for us to overlook.
"To you, O Lord, I lift up my soul." For some this might
seem like an echo from the *Sursum Corda* in the Anglican
communion service: "Lift up your hearts, we lift them up
unto the Lord." The original meaning of the word *nephesh*,
which is translated as "soul," was "breath" or "the breath of
life." Our life breath, our very being, we lift into the presence of God. In this line there is a sense of trust or daring
confidence that we may enter into the presence of the Holy
God of Israel as we gather for worship.

In Psalm 24, this is posed as a question: "Who shall as-
cend the hill of the Lord? / And who shall stand in his holy
place?" (v. 3). Who indeed. Psalm 24 continues, "Those
who have clean hands and pure hearts" (v. 4 NRSV). But
who among us truly has clean hands and a pure heart?

1. Unless otherwise noted, all Scripture quotations in this chapter are from the ESV.

Yet, in Psalm 25:1 the psalmist enters God's presence with confidence: "To you, O Lord, I lift up my soul." The context makes clear that this is not a sense of self-confidence or faith in our own righteousness. The psalmist goes on to pray that God might, in his mercy, overlook the sinfulness of the psalmist: "Remember not the sins of my youth or my transgressions; / according to your steadfast love remember me" (v. 7). This carries an echo of Isaiah 6:5, where the prophet is brought into the presence of God: "Woe is me! For I am lost; for I am a man of unclean lips, and I dwell in the midst of a people of unclean lips; for my eyes have seen the King, the Lord of hosts!" Our psalmist, with Isaiah, bears witness that as we come into the presence of God, the layers of concealment—the masks we put on—or the images we project are peeled away, and we stand before God as who we truly are. There is nothing hidden before God, and the more clearly we see God, the more clearly we begin to understand the ways in which we have rebelled against him.

Rather than displaying naïve or misplaced self-confidence, the psalmist declares that his confidence is in the Lord and his mercy: "Remember your mercy, O Lord, and your steadfast love, / for they have been from of old" (v. 6). In verse 10, which we have not looked at yet, the text says that "all the paths of the Lord are steadfast love and faithfulness." Ultimately, the psalmist's confidence is not in his righteousness or his actions but in the faithfulness of God. Grace is at the center of this psalm. Grace is the fundamental character of God. The covenant faithfulness of God means that our efforts, our endeavors, are never the basis of God's action toward us but, rather, are always a response to God's gracious and loving initiative.

In light of this grace, how can we not respond? The psalmist cries out, "Make me to know your ways, O Lord; / teach me your paths. / Lead me in your truth and teach me" (vv. 4–5). This psalm cries out for the speaker's whole life to be lived as a response to God, or indeed the church's whole life to be lived out with God. This thought brings us to the present time, when we are not able to gather together or be present to one another, when we cannot sing songs of praise. A livestreamed service is bittersweet, for even as we enjoy some of the elements of worship, our virtual gathering serves as a stark reminder that we are not able to truly worship *together*. And when we do gather, we must wear masks, a practice that is the antithesis of worship. Livestreamed worship carries something of the echo of our worship together, and we can hope that it will sharpen the hunger that soon we may be able truly to gather to enter into the presence of God, to lift up our souls to him. In the meanwhile, we wait, and we hope.

This sense of waiting is also a part of the psalm: "None who wait for you shall be put to shame" (v. 3); "for you I wait all the day long" (v. 5). While we cannot sing together, we can continue to speak the psalms together. For the psalms give voice to the character and nature of the Holy One and also give voice to our hopes and fears. Psalm 25 seems particularly appropriate for this time: it has been called both a psalm of lament and a psalm of confidence. In waiting, we know both lament and confidence.

Psalm 25 is one of eight acrostic psalms arranged according to the Hebrew alphabet. Scholars have suggested different reasons for using such a pattern. Perhaps it is written to facilitate communication, a didactic tool meant to teach others about God, or perhaps it offers a way of expressing something of the character of God. Some might suggest that the acrostic psalm is the ancient cousin or distant relation of the alliterative sermon, in which the preacher conveys the major points of a sermon by finding words that all begin with the same letter or sound. The intention in the alliterative sermon is that repetition and pattern might help the listener remember and apply the Sunday message. So, for example, a three-point sermon on prayer might be built on these three points: prayer requires patience, prayer is powerful, and prayer produces results. While that might guarantee a memorable sermon, it may be memorable for all the wrong reasons. The title of one blog article on preaching suggests, "Four things can happen when you alliterate, and four of them are bad."[2] More often than not, words are stretched in ways that confuse or frustrate the listener or, worse, belittle the meaning of the text. So, the intent in alliterative sermons may be to communicate effectively, but the result may be quite the opposite.

It is a stretch to see any important relation between the alliterative sermon and the acrostic psalm. It is true that the acrostic psalm may have an educational aspect, as the alliterative sermon does, but the main intentions behind these two forms are completely different. Whereas the alliterative sermon intends to help the listener remember and apply the message, the psalmist uses the acrostic as something of an artistic device to give voice to the wonder, beauty, and majesty of God. An acrostic pattern is not meant to convey a particular message or principle; it is a recognition that the way words are put together matters and that there is importance, not just in the way that they are written, but in the way they are heard. The Jesuit priest and poet Gerard Manly Hopkins reflected this same understanding in his poems. In a letter to the poet Robert

2. Sunukjian, "Four Things."

Bridges about one of his poems, Hopkins declared, "You must not slovenly read it with the eyes but with the ears."[3] Hopkins marked his poems with foot divisions, accents, and loops to indicate where the accent should fall and to enhance the sound and stress of each poem. He knew that to give expression to the truth and beauty of nature and the truth and beauty of God, we must use all the facilities of spoken language: rhythm, cadence, imagery. His use of echo, alliteration, repetition, and compressed syntax was meant to convey his understanding and experience in giving voice to the grandeur, mystery, and mercy of God. His poem "Pied Beauty" begins like this:

> Glory be to God for dappled things—
>> For skies of couple-colour as a brinded cow;
>>> For rose-moles all in stipple upon trout that swim;
> Fresh-firecoal chestnut-falls; finches' wings;
>> Landscape plotted and pieced—fold, fallow, and plough.[4]

We must learn to read the psalms with our ears as well as our eyes in order to enter into the cadence and voice of the psalms more fully. Like many of the psalms, Psalm 25 is not simply teaching us about God. It draws us into his presence in an encounter with God, that in such an encounter we might come to know him more fully.

Psalm 25 is a psalm for in-between times. It is a prayer or hymn of praise concerned not only with enlightenment but with strength. One intention is that as we wait in times of uncertainty and distress, we might know the ways of the Lord and walk in them so that we may sing his praise.

---

3 Gerard Manley Hopkins by Charlotte Barrett at http://writersinspire.org/content/gerard-manley-hopkins. Accessed June 15, 2021.

4. Hopkins, *The Poems of Gerald Manley Hopkins*, 69.

This brings me to say one more thing about this psalm. From the sixth century on, the Catholic Church sang the first verses of this psalm on the first Sunday of Advent, recognizing that it is a psalm of David, the penitent king, but that it also looks and points toward Jesus as the true King, the true mediator between God and humanity.

Augustine suggests that it is Christ himself who speaks in this psalm in the person of the church, for what is said has reference to the people turned toward God. In Christ, we enter with confidence into the very presence of God. Indeed, Christ himself is God's spoken Word, spoken with rhythm, cadence, and imagery, that we might hear and know that in him all God's promises are fulfilled.

Scripture: Psalm 25:1–8

Questions

1. How might the psalms help us to find our place in the midst of a crisis like the COVID pandemic?

2. The psalm speaks of our confidence to enter into the presence of God. For us as Christians, Christ is our confidence. How might we cultivate a sense of our privilege to enter into the presence of the Holy One of Israel?

3. How might the Psalms teach us to embrace attentively the richness of spoken language that helps us orient our praise toward God? What does it mean to read the Psalms with our ears as well as our eyes?

4. Augustine interpreted this psalm in the context of Christ. How does his interpretation help us, in our own reading of the Psalms, to see Christ as the one who prays these Psalms before the Father?

8

And David Says, "Sing!"

Catherine Sider-Hamilton

THERE IS A PAINTING that I love. It is *The Forerunners of Christ with Saints and Martyrs* by Fra Angelico, the monk who painted like an angel, and it is radiant.[1] In this artwork we see all the saints, old and new, black and brown and white, all of them going in procession together, wreathed in gold. There is John the Baptist front and center and King David beside him with his lyre; there are the prophets with their long white beards, several kneeling nuns, the child Agnes carrying the lamb, women and men old and young, every face distinctive, all of them somehow beautiful in front of their golden halos, dressed in their robes of rose and green and blue. It is the communion of saints.

> After this I looked, and behold a great crowd
> that no one could number, from every nation
> and tribe and people and tongue, standing be-
> fore the throne and before the Lamb. (Rev 7:9)

This is the communion of saints in their glory, and it seems a far cry from David in Psalm 34. Fra Angelico and

1. Angelico, *The Forerunners of Christ with Saints and Martyrs.*

Revelation give us the saints in their glory. But David has another word to say.

For it is David who speaks to us from the psalm. That is what the psalm superscription tells us. Before the psalm's first verse there is a note. This is the psalm of David, it says, "when he feigned madness before Abimelech, so that he drove him out, and he went away"[2]

David sings this psalm, but it is not the David of Fra Angelico's painting or of Revelation, the David robed in white with glory on his forehead. This is the David of 1 Samuel 21, alone and on the run. This is David cowering in the court of King Achish of Gath, with spittle running down his beard.

David has fled to Gath for refuge, but there the king's men say to the king, "Is this not David, the king of the land? Do they not sing of him, 'Saul has slain his thousands, but David his ten thousands?'" (1 Sam 21:11). David takes these words to heart, 1 Samuel 21:12 tells us, and is "very much afraid"—afraid for his life, for no king likes a rival. He is in Gath in the first place because Saul wants to kill him. Saul, too, heard the song—David has slain his ten thousands—and was not pleased. "Send and bring David to me," Saul the king said to Jonathan his son, "for he shall surely die" (1 Sam 20:31). But Jonathan loves David and warns him, and David flees. He leaves his home, his people, and his dearest friend. "[David] bowed three times [before Jonathan, his friend], and they kissed each other, and wept with each other; David wept the more. Then Jonathan said to David, 'Go in peace . . . ' [David] got up and left" (1 Sam 20:41–42).

---

2. Translations of scripture are from the NRSV; where they differ from the NRSV they are my own.

This is David alone and lonely, running for his life. And in the city in which he seeks refuge, he finds himself alone again, again in fear for his life. So, David "changed his behavior before them; he pretended to be mad." This is 1 Samuel 21:13, and it is, in substance, our psalm's superscription.

David sings this song alone in Gath, acting like a madman. This is the man God has chosen, David of the ruddy cheeks and bright eyes, David the giant-slayer, David the battle hero, David the man anointed to be king.

"Where is your word in this?" David could understandably ask his God. "Where are the promises?" he easily could wonder as he sits alone and lonely in Gath, scratching marks into the gate—in Gath, of all places. Gath is the land from which Goliath came, Goliath, Israel's enemy, the giant David has slain. It is some mark of David's desperation that he finds himself in this place. "Where is your word in this?" David could understandably ask his God.

But he sings, "I will bless the Lord" (Ps 34:1). "In all times I will bless him. His praise shall ever be in my mouth" (Ps 34:1). In this time of loneliness, David sings these words to the Lord. And he says, "The Lord is near to the brokenhearted" (v. 18). David blesses the Lord in his hard time; it is in the time of his affliction that he makes this song. "My soul boasts in the Lord," David says in v. 2.

"He acted like a madman," says 1 Samuel 21:13 (NIV), the verse that is quoted in this psalm's superscription. In Hebrew, "my soul boasts" (*tithallêl*) and "he acted like a madman" (*yithōlêl*) are different forms of the same root. The psalm thus draws together the time of David's affliction as we read in the psalm today and the time of his boast in the Lord as we read in the psalm today. And in David's song in the time of affliction, we hear the word of the saints. The Lord is near. It is not only in our glory that he wraps us around but in our desperation too. "The LORD is near to the brokenhearted" (v. 18), David sings, alone and lonely in Gath.

It is a good week—a good year—to hear his song. We know a little about loneliness in this era of COVID. I look at the four walls of my study in the morning, and I want to be just about anywhere else: somewhere, anywhere, just so long as there is another warm body. I miss the library! I am not sure I would ever have predicted that, but I do—the books, yes, but mostly the people, the small buzz of people around, clacking their laptop keys, turning pages, slurping coffee—just people being people. I miss the company even of strangers. Yet I have David, my husband; two of our children, who live in the city; and, on Sundays, the people of my church. Some of you have come this fall from faraway places to a strange city, to a new college, and the faces that you meet are digital or masked. You know a little bit about loneliness right now.

Out of his loneliness, David speaks to ours. In these words, in this psalm we sing, he speaks to us. We are not alone. How near David is to us in these words. It is the communion of saints. In our loneliness, David speaks to us, and he says, "The Lord is near to the brokenhearted."

The loneliness we experience today is a pointer. It is a pointer to David's loneliness and his song. The Lord is near. Even this hard thing, this COVID time, is caught up in the song of the saints. It is a song that rises in all times of trial. Jesus is clear about this: the life of the people who love the Lord is one that knows affliction. If our loneliness joins us to David in his song today, there is this blessing in it: it reminds us of David's greater loneliness. For there is something more to be said about David's loneliness. David is alone in Gath, hounded out of his home, for the sake of God's kingdom. David is sitting in a corner drooling, hiding in plain sight, because he is God's anointed, because he brings the reign of God. The kings of the earth, Saul and Achish and Herod after them, do not like this one bit. David is alone because he is God's servant in a world that does not want God. "Blessed are those who are persecuted for righteousness' sake," Jesus says, "for theirs is the kingdom of heaven" (Matt 5:10). This is the life of the saint. This is the life of the saint in the time of the world's kingdoms. This David drooling in a corner in fear for his life *is* that David crowned in glory in Fra Angelico's golden painting. They are the same person. This is the glory of the saint. In this world, the glory of the saint cannot be separated from the cross. In the Beatitudes (Matt 5:1–12), Jesus on that mountain in Galilee is talking about David. Jesus is taking up David's song; he is giving it to all of us, to all who follow him, to all the saints. He is making David's song the song of the kingdom.

> Blessed are the poor in spirit, for theirs is the kingdom of heaven. (Matt 5:3)

> The Lord . . . will save those whose spirits are crushed. (Ps 34:18)

> Blessed are the humble. (Matt 5:5 CSB)

> Let the humble hear and rejoice. (Ps 34:2)

Jesus sings again David's song, the song of the brokenhearted, the song of those who suffer for the kingdom's sake. Jesus speaks David's song here at the beginning of his ministry, to his disciples gathered around. It is the Sermon on the Mount; it is the charter of the kingdom of heaven; it is the song of the saints.

It is also Jesus' own song. Jesus, son of David, will also be alone. It is to a cross that his journey leads. Jesus will be alone like David for the kingdom's sake. "My God, my God, why have you forsaken me?" (Mark 15:34; Matt 27:46; also Ps 22:1). When he is lifted up on that cross, we will no longer be alone forever. "The angel of the Lord encamps / around those who fear him" (Ps 34:7). He encamps around us like a mighty army.

David's song—David's loneliness for the kingdom's sake—finds an answer in Jesus Christ. The righteous cry, David says, and the Lord will deliver them (Ps 34:17). This is what the saints know. It is why David sings in his time of trouble. It is why all Fra Angelico's saints are radiant, David hunted in Gath, John the Baptist beheaded, Agnes slaughtered at twelve years old for righteousness' sake. They are all radiant. For the Lord is near. He is near in Jesus Christ our Lord.

"He will keep safe all our bones; not one of them shall be broken" (Ps 34:20). With his own bones, with his pierced feet, Jesus makes this pledge. That is why David sings. That is why we sing with him today. With him, and with all the saints, we lift up our song. It is a mighty chorus, black and brown and white, woman and man and child, old and young, singing David's song, handing it on, voice by voice and scroll by scroll and prayer by prayer—broken heart by broken heart—in all the days of Israel and all the days of the church, singing David's song, handing it on together. It is the communion of saints.

"These are they," an elder in Revelation says, who have dipped their robes "in the blood of the Lamb" (7:14). The life of the saint lies in the shadow of the cross.

And David says, "Sing!" And the saints say, "Sing!" And the Lamb upon the throne says, "Sing!"

Look upon him, Christ crucified, Christ the King. Look upon him and be radiant.

Scripture: Psalm 34

Questions

1. Under what circumstances did David write Psalm 34?

2. Do you think David in Psalm 34 is the blessed one Jesus refers to in the Beatitudes? Why?

3. Where is Jesus in this year of COVID?

4. "The life of the saint lies in the shadow of the cross." What do you think it means for us to be saints?

9

Restoration

Thomas Power

SOME YEARS AGO, OUR family came into possession of an old piece of furniture, an antique dining-room buffet or dresser. We had to decide whether it was beyond repair, whether the expense involved was worth it for what we would get in the end, and whether we were willing to wait for the lengthy job to be done instead of opting for the convenience and cheaper cost of buying something new. In the end, enamored by the beauty of old things, we decided to get the dresser restored.

Now, I am not a handyman, but I respect those who do have such skills, in this case with furniture restoration. Observing the different stages of the work led me to appreciate what is involved in such a task. First, there has to be an identification and assessment of what the exact *problem* is before any repairs are undertaken. Otherwise, the work can be misdirected and energies wasted. Second, there has to be a clear vision of the desired outcome, what the finished *product* will look like. If not, then the work is elusive and misplaced. Third, to achieve a good result, there has to be close attention to detail and precision all along in the *process*. This involves sanding, gluing, staining, and pointing, with the use of special tools. There cannot be any shortcuts, though the job is often exacting and painful. Finally, there has to be immense *patience*, given the complexity of the job, along with the commitment to persevere and attain the desired finished product. Otherwise, setbacks and unexpected challenges can frustrate the entire project.

In summary, in any work of restoration, you have to know the problem, keep the end product in view, pay attention to detail, and be patient during the process. How might this analogy of furniture restoration help us with understanding Psalm 80? As in the case of the dresser, let us start with identifying the problem as it is revealed to us.

Problem: Oppression and Abandonment

The psalm tells us about Israel's problems, the main one being that it is oppressed by enemies. In fact, throughout its history, Israel was a much-conquered people with many oppressors. At this particular time, the northern state of Israel, the house of Joseph, here represented by mention of Ephraim, Benjamin, and Manasseh, has been plundered by Assyria, with many exiled as a result. What is more, these problems of oppression seem greater and more acute when they are contrasted with Israel's preceding condition. Previously, the vine of Israel was healthy and prosperous due to God's nurture. To remind us of this, we are given a short history lesson:

> You brought a vine out of Egypt;
>> you drove out the nations and planted it.
> You cleared the ground for it,
>> and it took root and filled the land.

The mountains were covered with its shade,
    the mighty cedars with its branches.
It sent out its boughs to the sea,
    its shoots as far as the River. (vv. 8–11)[1]

In this psalm, the nation of Israel, which God has brought out of Egypt, is referred to as the vine. Israel is also called the "son you have raised up for yourself," the "man at your right hand," and the "son of man you have raised up for yourself" (vv. 15, 17). These different phrases for the vine are a play on the name "Benjamin," which means "son of the right hand" (see v. 2). Only by God's intervention was the vine transplanted from Egypt and then allowed to prosper, as shown here by the extent of the territory given to Israel by God.

But now this healthy and prosperous state is ravaged and plundered as a result of conquest by enemies:

All who pass by pick its grapes . . . (v. 12)
Boars from the forest ravage it
    and the creatures of the field feed on it . . . (v. 13)
Your vine is cut down, it is burned with fire. (v. 16)

The careful planting and cultivation of the vineyard has resulted in fire instead of fruit. The vine that previously spread, was productive, and gave protection is now plundered by enemies and destroyed. What is worse, not only is Israel conquered, but it is laughed at by its enemies: "You have made us an object of derision to our neighbors, / and our enemies mock us" (v. 6 NIV).

In this situation the psalmist is perplexed. He asks why God, who formed and prospered a people for himself, now

1. Unless otherwise noted, all Scripture quotations in this chapter are from the NIV 1984. Note that the abbreviation "NIV," when used without a year after it, refers to the NIV 2011.

seems to have abandoned them. What has happened to the deliverance they knew when they left Egypt, the sustenance they received in the wilderness, the presence of God they experienced when they conquered the promised land? Why does God no longer care for them, his vine (v. 8)?

All this is bad enough, but there is another problem: God is unresponsive to prayer, seemingly angry, and gives only sorrow. When they seek his answer, even their prayers seem to anger him. Their sense of alienation from God is very great: "How long will your anger smolder against the prayers of your people?" (v. 4)

God has now given them tears to eat and tears to drink rather than the bread of angels and water from the rock:

"You have fed them with the bread of tears;

　you have made them drink tears by the bowlful." (v. 5)

Instead of water and manna, why does God now give them tears?

To them, it all has the appearance of undeserved punishment. Here, then, is the problem: oppression and mocking from enemies are signs that God has abandoned his vineyard.

Outcome: Saved

If oppression by enemies and abandonment by God are the problem, then what is the vision held out as the desired resolution? What, in this communal lament, does the psalmist see as a solution to Israel's problems? In other words, as was asked in the case of the dresser, what should the finished product be? When the problems are addressed, when everything is put right, what should things look like?

Recall that a basic trait of all the Psalms is expression of the need to be put right with God. In Psalm 80 this is expressed in the psalmist's declared desire to be saved. The phrase "that we may be saved" is repeated three times in verses 3, 7, and 19. To be saved is the goal, the end product, the desired outcome. How, then, is it to be reached? What is the process?

Process: God Intervenes

The psalmist makes clear repeatedly that salvation is to come through the action and intervention of God. It is to God that a series of requests or pleas are addressed.

1. "Hear," the first word in the psalm (v. 1).

2. "Awaken your might" (v. 2), a call for God to use his power.

3. "Make your face shine upon us" (v. 3), repeated twice (vv. 7, 19), a call to God to show favor to his people.

4. "Return," "look down," "watch over" (v. 14), a plea for God's protection.

All these pleas—"hear," "awaken," "shine," "return"—conclude with the key solution to Israel's problems: restoration. It is asked for three times, with increasing intensity:

"Restore us, O God" (v. 3).

"Restore us, O God Almighty" (v. 7).

"Restore us, O Lord God Almighty." (v.19)

"Hear," "awaken," "shine," "return," and "restore" are like the glues and materials used by the furniture restorer. Here God is the restorer. Israel cannot be her own savior. The prayer relies entirely on what God can do: only he can restore his people and cause them to turn back to him. Only he can welcome them back with a shining face, showing his pleasure in them, with the assurance that they are saved.

So, we have identified Israel's problem (abandonment by God, oppression by enemies), we have seen what the desired outcome is (being saved), and we have identified how this is to be achieved (through restoration). In all this, God the restorer is patient, an attribute that has characterized his relationship with the nation of Israel ever since it began, with the calling of Abraham.

Application

Currently, we are in the midst of a pandemic. The COVID virus is an oppressive and a seemingly relentless enemy. It is all around. There is vacancy, isolation, and abandonment. We have many questions, like Where is God in the midst of this pandemic? What are we to do in our abandonment? There are no easy or satisfying answers to such wrenching questions. But not having the answers, waiting, pleading, and crying out to God even in our sorrow, anger, and doubt are part of the answer.

Psalm 80 permits us to question God's abandonment and absence, to confess our disillusionment and disappointments with life and with God. It shows us that it is legitimate for us to plead to the Lord: "hear," "awaken," "shine your face," "restore" are all things we can say in faith and hope.

As God's people, we can come to him simply pleading our own need and the needs of the world. Such is his grace and our privilege. Like Israel, we can call on God to do for us what we cannot do for ourselves, and we do so in the knowledge that the initiative, as in all aspects of salvation, lies with God alone.

Advent is an appropriate time to mourn and to rage against the seeming absence of God. So, at the outset of this Advent season, as we await the coming of the Shepherd of Israel, let us cry out in faith and hope with the psalmist: "Restore us, O LORD God Almighty; / make your face shine upon us, / that we may be saved" (v. 19).

Scripture: Psalm 80

Questions

1. What does God need to do in your life?

2. How badly do you want God to restore you?

3. What would the result look like?

10

Hope and Prayer amid Displacement

Glen Taylor

I recently read a poem whose message was almost as relevant to someone living in the time of COVID as it was to someone living in the late exilic or postexilic period in which the bulk of Psalm 106 was written.

To get a better picture of how Psalm 106 relates to us here and now, we need briefly to review its overall structure. This forty-eight-verse-long psalm begins and ends with a call to praise. Verse 1 says, "Praise the Lord. / Give thanks to the Lord, for he is good; / his love endures forever," whereas verse 48 reads, "Praise be to the Lord, the God of Israel, / from everlasting to everlasting. / Let all the people say "Amen." / Praise the Lord."[1] So, there is a beginning and an ending call for praise. A few verses from the beginning of the psalm, and one verse before the final one, we find a cry for God to intervene, beginning with "Remember me, Lord," in verse 4 and ending with "Save us, Lord our God" in verse 47. So, the second part of our structure highlights a cry for help.

1. Unless otherwise noted, all Scripture quotations in this chapter are from the NIV.

It might just make you hungry, but think of the praise and call for help as the bread on the top and bottom of a sandwich, but one with four rather than two pieces of bread: praise, cry for intervention, middle, cry for intervention, and praise. And what lies in the middle? A thick, meaty rehearsal of God's acts of salvation in the past, accompanied by a recounting of Israel's acts of rebellion at pretty much every stage of God's history of salvation.

It is time now to partake of our sandwich, and as we do so, we will ponder what drawing nourishment from this divinely inspired meal means during a time of pandemic. Because eating during COVID is not the same as during normal time—try eating in a restaurant with a mask on—we are going to set the bread parts aside for a moment and eat the middle first. Actually, since we cannot eat in restaurants right now, we shall partake of this meal as a takeout; and from it we shall "take away" three edifying thoughts.

The first concerns the middle part, which is the historical narrative beginning in verse 6 and ending in verse 46. In this section, which reads like a tragicomic documentary, God saves his people over and over again and performs dramatic miracles such as the parting of the sea and the drawing of water from a rock, and Israel ignores God, forgets him, puts him to the test, or snubs him. Over and over again, God puts on a show, only for Israel to respond in disobedience and sin, though there are a few times when Moses and Phinehas do the right thing. We need venture no further than verse 7 to see this pattern exemplified and encapsulated in a single verse. It reads, "When our ancestors were in Egypt, *your miracles provoked no thought; the people did not remember your many kindnesses, and they rebelled* by the sea, the Red Sea" (paraphrased from the

NIV, order changed slightly to highlight the point, emphasis added).

Notice how they rebel by the Red Sea, also known as the "Reed Sea," which God split in half so they could walk across on dry ground. How could they choose to rebel here of all places? Well, it is a nice setting for rebellion: at least until recently, the beaches were nice and dry, with strong, moderating breezes. There were lots of interesting things to see: Egyptian spears, shiny helmets wafting ashore as the sun sets. Other rebels will wait for a palm desert–like setting to shun God; you know, wait until you get thirsty, and then, when he installs a big water tap in a dry rock, charge him with being late; or when he miraculously provides quail, say, "Excuse me, I am a vegan." It is laughable but also pathetic and, of course, all too typical of—well, us.

Anchoring this tug of war between the people, who move away from God, and God, who is pulling them back, is an Archimedean point, which is the covenant, in which God promises blessing for obedience and punishment for sin. Yes, punishment for sin.

So, what does this have to do with COVID? Well, if *we* are not asking whether this epidemic is a punishment for sin, *others* are. And one can find support for an affirmative answer here and in other Deuteronomistic-type Scriptures that support this theology; one example comes from Psalm 106:14–15.

> In the desert they gave in to their craving;
>> in the wilderness they put God to the test.
> So he gave them what they asked for,
> [then] sent a wasting disease among them. (NIV[2])

2. In verse 15 the NIV has "but" instead of my added "then," which owes to the JPS Tanakh (1985).

In many parts of the world today Christians believe that bad things happen to people for only one reason: because they have sinned.

When I first came to Toronto in 1987, I was asked by the Museum of the History of Medicine to give a lecture on "plagues and pestilence" in the Bible. I argued, and still do, that there is a connection between calamity and human sin in biblical understanding but that Jesus, in particular, warned his followers against associating any calamity that might befall someone with *that person's individual sin.*[3] Now, the apostle Paul makes it clear that illness does befall some people because of their own sin (1 Cor 11:30), but that is not a judgment we are to make or even to think; remember Job, and leave that judgment alone to God—or, in Paul's case, to him under the direct inspiration of the Spirit—to say. Do not go there.

Repentance

So, what are we to take away from this in light of the current pandemic? Verse 6, which I have omitted until now, provides a suggestion: the psalmist writes, "We have sinned, even as our ancestors did; / we have done wrong and acted wickedly." The psalmist points the finger at the covenant community, and not even the psalmist is excluded. Does

3. This does not mean that there is never a one-to-one connection between a person's sin and an ill that befalls them. In addition to calling for repentance from the person posing the connection, Jesus is making the point that it is never up to us to make that determination. That is presumably between God and the person, unless that person be a scriptural prophet, apostle, or the like. Cf. John 9:1, concerning which it might nevertheless be argued that the sin of the blind man was, in this unique instance, an occasion for the manifestation of God's glory.

this mean we should blame ourselves for COVID? That is not what I am saying, and it certainly is not a good idea for any of us who are too hard on ourselves already. But it sure beats blaming God alone, independent of human sin. What I am saying is that a time like this ought naturally to lead us to self-examination, not to blame ourselves or anyone else specifically, but to consider what sins we might have committed (not that caused the pandemic, but in general) and to name, confess, and repent of them. Let me say that again: *a time like this ought naturally to lead us to self-examination, not to blame ourselves or anyone else specifically, but to consider what sins we might have committed (not that caused the pandemic, but in general) and to name, confess, and repent of them.* Jesus himself teaches as much in Luke 13. He gives a firm no to the idea that certain Galileans "whose blood Pilate had mixed with their sacrifices" "were worse sinners than all the other Galileans because they suffered this way" (vv. 1–2), and he says the same thing of "those eighteen who died when the tower in Siloam fell on them" (v. 4). Then Jesus says something surprising, at least to me. He says, "I tell you, no! But unless you repent, you too will all perish" (v. 5).

Here, Jesus' 'takeaway' from two tragedies which, like COVID, were all over the news, was to repent. Why? Because, Jesus continues, unless we repent of our sins, we will end up like the worst human casualties of COVID: dead; put simply, without repentance, the future divine judgment for actually committed sins will kill us. This is scary. Although it may be Jesus' intention in this passage, my purpose here is not to instill fear—there is enough fear-mongering amid this pandemic already—but to remind us of the importance of confession and repentance of sin. So, if we are smart enough to mask up and practice social distancing due to COVID, we should be no less smart in taking precautions for the coming pandemic of the divine judgment. And what would those precautions be? Right now, whether for the first time or not, you can trust in Jesus and in the saving power of his death for us, for you and me, on the cross. Part of the way we do this is by repenting of our sin, knowing that as we do so, his cross shields us from the calamity of condemnation on the last day. For that pandemic yet to come, then, do not don your mask of self-righteousness; take it off and confess Jesus as the Lord you need to atone for your many sins; and do not wash your hands, but get dirt on your knees by kneeling in humble submission to God's overwhelming love and power to save, exemplified so abundantly in our psalm.[4]

Few things run against the grain of our culture more than acknowledging sin and repenting of it before a holy and loving God. God help us to do these very things!

Fellowship

If our first takeaway is to use COVID as an occasion for self-examination and repentance, the second is this: *Ask God to bring us together again into the full joy and fellowship of his church.* Cry out to him for deliverance. Remember what verses 4 and 47 say, respectively: "Remember me, LORD," and "Save us, LORD our God." What is it that the psalmist most wants God to save him from? Allow me to answer that question with an illustration.

4. There follows, from this central section, another takeaway truth, and it lies in the observation that the psalmist, though not denying his own personhood, associates himself inextricably with the covenant community as a whole. In short, the covenant community is comprised of individuals, none of whom think of themselves apart from the whole of which they are a part.

When one of my colleagues first walked into this chapel to preach a few weeks ago, he said he was taken aback by emotions, including gladness for being here again and sadness over seeing so few allowed in chapel. But perhaps most of all, he longed for all of us to be here, worshipping again. So long as COVID keeps us from worshipping together in person, something is very wrong.

Our psalmist knew what it was like to worship apart from his community. It was not a biological foe that had removed him from his community, but rather a foreign army. Either way, the effect is the same: a longing to regather in our places of worship. Look again at the rest of what verses 4 (and now 5) and 47 cry out for: After "Remember me, LORD" (v. 4) and some further wording, we read the reason for his cry: "that I *may enjoy the prosperity of your chosen ones,* / that I *may share in the joy of your nation* / and [*glory in your very own people*]" (v. 5 NIV, emphasis added, altered text taken from the JPS Tanakh). And in verse 47, after "Save us, LORD our God," again we find the hope: "gather us from the nations"! The psalmist, like us, is longing to experience the joys of God's kingdom while worshipping once again—without social distancing, right beside his brothers and sisters. Psalm 106 implicitly invites us to long for the same: reunion, and soon.

I worry that not everyone feels the same about reuniting. Just last week I talked to a woman who told me she prefers staying at home to "watch church." She said she does not miss going to church at all! God forbid that attitude to take hold; God forbid that the convenience of Zoom and the broken habit of "going to church" remove our desire to regather physically in a place of worship. May we pray with genuineness and sincerity to be reunited to "share the joy of Your nation," and "glory in Your very own people" (v. 5 JPS Tanakh).

Let me review. The first takeaway had to do with the occasion COVID provides for us to take stock of our lives, and to confess and repent of true sin. The second takeaway was an invitation to pray for our isolation to end. And now, in what follows, is the third takeaway: a reminder of the primacy and privilege of praise in corporate worship.

Praise

Three thoughts come to mind on praise. First, regardless of where we are, praise is primary; it is the direction in which the whole book of Psalms is leading us. Second, praise in the Old Testament is always corporate; a helpful reminder of this is that the Hebrew word for praise, Hallelujah, is an imperative verb *in the plural*. Zoom praise is fine *for now*. And third, praise is more than what rattles off our tongues, but includes living a righteous life. Verses 2–3 remind us of this in asking, "Who can proclaim the mighty acts of the LORD, / or fully declare his praise?" (v. 2). The answer that implicitly follows is this: "those who act justly, / who always do what is right" (v. 3). As one commentator has put it, "to show forth all his praise will take lives as well as lips."[5]

Let me conclude with the words that end our psalm and that form the ending to this whole section of the book of Psalms:

Praise be to the Lord, the God of Israel,
    from everlasting to everlasting.
Let all the people say, "Amen!"
Praise the Lord.

Scripture: Psalm 106

5. Kidner, *Psalms 73–50*, 378.

Questions

1. Is there any connection between calamity and human sin in biblical understanding? To whom, in this sermon, does the author intend to entrust that judgment?

2. What does the author suggest doing in this pandemic time instead of blaming ourselves or anyone else specifically?

3. The author says, "If we are smart enough to mask up and practice social distancing due to COVID, we should be no less smart in taking precautions for the coming pandemic of the divine judgment." What would those precautions be?

4. Before the pandemic, did you regard praise as having primacy and privilege in corporate worship?

11

The Malnourishment of Separation

David Kupp

ADVENT 2020 BEGAN ABOUT ten months after the first COVID case in Ontario was reported, at Sunnybrook Hospital in Toronto on Jan 27. An Angus Reid poll in early December 2020 amply demonstrated Canadians' growing preoccupation with the morose and the maudlin. Here are the things that most absorbed our minds during Advent:[1]

1. According to Angus Reid's poll, four in five Canadians were concerned about their friends and family becoming sick.

2. Most Canadians had greatly reduced their social circles, a strange feature of good citizenship now rewarded and applauded.

3. We had also become a nation of apocalyptic expectations—three-quarters of Canadians expected that the worst was yet to come.

4. 84 percent believed that economic conditions would decline further.

1. Angus Reid Institute,"Covid Christmas".

5. The poll also noted that in 1988, 27 percent of Canadians said that Christmas is primarily a religious occasion. At the time of the poll, that count had dropped by nearly two-thirds, to 10 percent of Canadians. Among the 10 percent who still considered Christmas religious, less than half intended to follow a service online. Younger observers were more likely simply to use an app for prayer or meditation.

In light of our text and this pandemic moment of collisions in time and events, I am not sure what to title this meditation. Above all, we each sense a discernible and accelerated thinning of our connectivity and our relational reserves—a thinning of the social and spiritual capital of our life together. As church and community leaders, and capacity builders, this is of direct concern to all of us. So perhaps this title would be best: "The Malnourishment of Separation."

The Psalms have been around for a couple dozen centuries, with interpretive traditions being suggestive of a range of authors and a gradual emergence over a long period of development. The Psalms reflect a variety of Jewish cultic, festival, agrarian, and theo-political settings. The chanting, praying, and singing of these prayers and poems have seen far better and far worse times than our own. We have also been learning that more than any other text of the Jewish Scriptures, the Psalms speak directly to those who recite and sing them. The psalmists, unlike the prophets, require neither that we know who they are nor that we understand precisely their *Sitz im Leben*, their socio-historical contexts. The Psalms envelop us with their frequently vivid and emotional tapestries of relationships between God, humans, and creation. Ellen Davis says this:

> Psalms are addressed to the heart, which in the
> metaphorical physiology of the Bible is the or-
> gan of imagination, thought, feeling, and will;
> [the heart] is also the locus of faith and personal
> commitment, the faculty whereby humans make
> a real connection with God.[2]

It is natural and important, then, to sing and pray these songs and poems as liturgies of the heart that speak about the ordinary, not detached and lofty spirituality. The psalmists speak openly and continually of the things that threaten a healthy relationship with God, each other, and creation. Across all the collections within the psalter, every gathered congregation, Jewish and Christian, encounters tangible moments of joy and despair, hope and lamentation, flourishing and suffering. The psalter may be mostly limited to singing, chanting, and praying, but it signifies real ancient worlds of complexity, danger, and possibility, with all their political, economic, and agrarian features.

When we read Psalm 85 carefully, it manages to distinguish itself among the psalms on at least a couple of fronts. One is its combination of grateful recollection, lament, listening, pleading for restoration, praise, and possibly even ecstatic hope by the end. Another is its final stanza, which leaves us with a soaring and enigmatic cry for cosmic *shalom*, where God and creation and heaven and earth work together once again in full harmony.

Where do I find the "malnourishment of separation" in Psalm 85? Most basically, there is physical malnutrition, with its social and economic consequences, arising from the failure of the land. This is an agrarian people, and when drought comes, subsistence farmers have far less to eat between harvests. Even the precious seeds they stored for the

2. Davis, *Opening Israel's Scriptures*, 312.

next planting may be sacrificed for the sake of a meal today. For farmers practicing animal husbandry, drought and ancient diseases like rinderpest can decimate their herds, leaving children and households without milk, meat, and fuel for the fire. Vulnerable agrarians quickly become vassals of the local lender, borrowing against next season's production for the sake of survival today. The psalmist's plea for renewal is thus not simply focused on the clan's spiritual relationship with God but is fully grounded in the soil, the regeneration of the land, and questions of produce, blessing, fertility, and well-being.[3]

The Lord will give what is good,
    and our land will yield its increase.[4]

So, the ecology of hunger in Psalm 85 is whole, for everything is connected in the divine economy of *shalom*. In the recollections and lament of 85:1–6, we see a picture of:

- The decline and failure of the land
- The spiritual misadventures of the people
- The experience of God's anger and wrath
- A downward multigenerational spiral
- The joyless existence of communities amidst social and spiritual depression

Here is the complication: Psalm 85 tells us that this is not Israel's first rodeo. This is not the first time the people of God find themselves amidst socioeconomic, ecological, and spiritual collapse. There is a pattern, which some commentators describe as orientation, disorientation, reorientation.

3. Brueggemann, *Theology of the Old Testament*, 482.

4. Unless otherwise noted, all Scripture quotations in this chapter are from the ESV.

There can be long-term consequences to repeating the cycle, to developing a pattern of chronic malnutrition, whether physical, social, or spiritual. From my experience in the world of international development, I believe that child malnutrition delivers increasingly serious consequences when it is repeated and chronic, when it progresses from (1) temporary hunger to (2) malnourishment to (3) wasting to (4) stunting.

Children with low weight for their age exhibit stunting. This results from chronic or recurrent malnutrition, which is associated with poverty, is frequently linked with the poor health and nutrition of the mother, and often comes with recurrent illness. Stunting is serious; its impacts can be permanent. These children, if they survive, become adults with irreversibly diminished physical and cognitive development. The window of time is narrow for thwarting the life-long impacts of stunting.

Globally, the World Food Program tells us, before the COVID pandemic more than 21 percent of children under five were stunted. There is a long list of indicators of physical stunting through malnutrition. In light of Psalm 85 we might think about how some of these indicators apply to social and spiritual malnutrition:

- The stunted child has a stature more than two standard deviations below median.
- She lives in a chronically malnourished household.
- Her immune system is weak.
- She exhibits impaired brain function.
- She is listless.
- She is uninterested in school or being with others.
- She has diminished strength and endurance.

In reading Psalm 85, I wonder what stunting, what permanent scar tissue results from the repeated rise, fall, and recovery of the spiritual, social, and ecological health of God's people.

The questions then become more directly our own:

- What indicators of stunting emerge in the body of any community that sees these repeated generational patterns?

- In what ways are malnutrition and Psalm 85 a window into our own current forms of social and spiritual hunger and malnutrition in the social distancing of this pandemic?

- What might Psalm 85 indicate about God's plans for our post-pandemic community revitalization?

- How are we to renourish and rethicken our social and spiritual capital together?

- How do we more fully comprehend and articulate the long-term impacts of excess digitization?

- Does our previous and current overindulgence in digitization speak to a related and perverse version of spiritual and social malnutrition, in two directions—deprivation of the rich social nutrition of in-person relationships and the accompanied bloating of digital obesity?

On this question of Psalm 85 and post-pandemic community renewal, I cannot resist a reference to *Babette's Feast*, a Danish book and film by Isak Dinesen, otherwise known as Karen Blixen. The film has, for more than thirty years, been a standout among the explorations of theology and film.[5] *Babette's Feast* has been plumbed and

5. Vaux, "Letters on Better Movies," 71.

investigated for its biblical exposition, feminist theology, liberation theology, intentional ascetic community practices, multiple dimensions of love, Danish church history, and more. I also hear that the film has become the favorite of Pope Francis, who has spoken and written of it.

For those of you who are as yet uninitiated into *Babette's Feast*, we arrive on the gray west coast of Denmark, in Jutland, in the nineteenth century. Two pious spinster sisters preside over a tiny Lutheran sect founded by their rigid, now-departed pastor and father. Their little hamlet of faith is dwindling into a joyless Puritanism concerned with rules and the avoidance of any pleasure.

But with the mysterious arrival of Babette, a refugee from French civil conflict, the tiny community slowly begins to change. After years of quiet service, Babette convinces them to try something other than their daily diet of boiled codfish and ale bread, and voila! One of the greatest (theological) food films is born. Babette's feast scandalizes, delights, awakens, and ultimately resurrects this moribund community of miserable believers.

Many observers have seen *Babette's Feast* as no less than a picture of the cosmic Eucharist, the great banquet of Christ, which includes redeemed people gathered from across time and space. For me, the pinnacle, the breaking open of *Babette's Feast*, comes in the dinner speech by Major Lorens, with his employment of the final words of Psalm 85.[6]

There is a palpable life cycle in community experience that speaks to our hunger for divine presence and to the extraordinary malnutrition that distance from others now imposes on community members, neighbors, colleagues, and friends. Each of us and creation itself are called to mediate the presence of God to each other. Paul's

6. Farrer, "Babette's Feast," video clip #4.

analogy of the body and its parts and Jesus' metaphor of
the vine and branches call us to break the repeated—and
now accelerated—pattern of distancing. Notably, this pattern of social distancing began to define us in ways that
were fragmented, disparate, and distracted long prior to
the arrival of COVID. Amidst this growing urban plague of
twenty-first-century loneliness, COVID is an *apokalupsis*,
a revelation, of these fissures and cracks that have already
begun amongst us in our practice and are now widened
and gaping dangerously.

I am encouraged by my belief that Psalm 85 can help
us with diagnosis and a post-pandemic vision. But the vision comes with requirements—that we listen and do not
turn to folly (v. 8) and that we understand our God as loving but also righteous. In the face of our human arrogance
and failure to listen, this God, the psalmist says, is capable
of "fierce anger" (v. 3 NIV).

In hope of restoration, all of the familiar covenantal
vocabulary is uniquely woven together in Psalm 85, with
several of the terms repeated and combined:

- *shalom*
- justice
- the land
- faithfulness
- steadfast love
- righteousness
- salvation.

Verses 10–13 comprise this psalm's lyrical gem, antic-
ipating the time—the post-pandemic time—when heaven
and earth and neighborhoods and the land will again be in
full harmony. These call for the repeated declaration by the

people of God then and now, reaching for the promise of restored togetherness.

> Steadfast love and faithfulness [will] meet;
>> righteousness and peace [will] kiss each other.
> Faithfulness [will spring] up from the ground,
>> and righteousness [will look] down from the sky.
> Yes, the LORD will give what is good,
>> and our land will yield its increase.
> Righteousness will go before him
>> and will make [a path for his steps].

The opposite of formation is deformation—the result of long-term malnutrition. Let us seek the Spirit's wisdom in this ancient psalm. May we understand in the days to come how to re-nourish, revive, and restore our wasting communities, churches, and organizations for the renewal of his kingdom.

Scripture: Psalm 85

Questions

1. How might you see the experience of your household this past year within this psalm's cycle of orientation, disorientation, and reorientation?

2. How does this psalm speak to your own community's current malnourishment?

3. What poem, song, or prayer might you pen in which God "speak[s] peace" to the people, and "dwell[s] in our land" and neighborhood (vv. 8–9)?

12

Remembering and Passing on the Unabridged Story of God

MARION TAYLOR

TODAY WE ARE CALLED to remember.[1] What Canadians now call Remembrance Day and Americans celebrate as Veterans Day began as Armistice Day more than a hundred years ago. It has become a day to honor the fallen and veterans and also to remember the horror of war and the importance of embracing peace.

Psalm 78, which is one of Asaph's psalms, also calls us to remember. It is a long psalm that rehearses Israel's history. Its seventy-two verses take between seven and nine minutes to read aloud.

Psalm 78 begins by setting out its purpose: in beautiful synonymous parallelism, the psalmist says, "Give ear . . . to my teaching; / incline your ears to the words of my mouth (v. 1). But what are the words we are called to listen to? Unexpectedly, the next verse tells us that the psalmist is going to speak a *mashal. Mashal* is the Hebrew word for "proverb," "riddle," "parable," or "instruction." The parallel

1. This meditation was originally prepared as a sermon that was delivered on November 11.

line in verse 2b explains that this particular *mashal* concerns the dark or mysterious enigmas from earlier times that his ancestors remembered and passed on. This *mashal* is not designed to entertain but rather to teach, to instruct, and to help us remember the past so that we can pass this information on to the next generations.

The theme of remembering is not new in the Old Testament. At the end of the flood story in Genesis 9:15–16, we read that when God sees the bow, or rainbow, in the clouds, he promises to remember the everlasting covenant he has established with every living creature and never again to destroy all flesh with the flood.

The theme of *not* remembering is also raised in the book of Genesis. After Joseph interprets the dreams of Pharaoh's chief baker and cupbearer, he specifically asks the cupbearer to remember him and show him kindness by mentioning him to Pharaoh so that he can get out of prison. But the narrator tells us twice in ch. 40 that the ungrateful cupbearer does not remember Joseph. Instead, he forgets him, meaning that Joseph remains in prison for another two years (v. 23).

The theme of remembering *and not forgetting* continues into Exodus, where we read in 6:5 that God hears the groaning of his enslaved people in Egypt and *remembers* his covenant. This remembering, of course, precipitates the eventual release of Israel from Egyptian bondage. The theme of remembering and not forgetting is also specifically associated with the saving acts of God and with the Sinai covenant that God's people commit themselves to remember. Repeatedly in Scripture, God's people are asked to *remember* what God has done for them and to remember their commitment to follow the prescriptions of the covenant. This twofold remembering is also found in Deuteronomy 8, where Moses calls Israel to "remember how the LORD your God led you all the way in the wilderness these forty years, to humble and test you in order to know what was in your heart, whether or not you would keep his commands," and to remember by observing "the commands of the LORD your God, walking in obedience to him and revering him" (vv. 2, 6 NIV).[2]

However, we all know that God's people were not good at remembering. Stories of their failures to remember what God had done for them and of their more blatant covenant-breaking dominate the Old Testament. The refrain in the book of Judges is a case in point: "In those days there was no king in Israel; all the people did what was right in their own eyes." (Judg 21:25). Jeremiah later describes the anguish of God's faithless in exile who "have perverted their way . . . [and] forgotten the LORD their God" (Jer 3:21 ESV).

So, the theme of remembering featured in Psalm 78 is not unique. It actually dominates much of Scripture. In this psalm, the psalmist calls us to remember what God has done for us and to recall the stories of our ancestors' responses to God's acts. He does this because he believes that remembering is an essential part of our identity as God's covenant people.

But remembering what God has done for us is not enough. In verses 4–7, we learn that we are to pass on what we have heard and what we know to the next generation. We are to teach God's glorious deeds and wonders and decrees to the next generation, which is then able to pass this knowledge on to the children who are yet unborn. The children can then rise up and, in turn, teach their children,

2. Unless otherwise noted, all Scripture quotations in this chapter are from the NRSV.

who will place their hope in God and not forget his acts, but instead keep his commandments.

Verses 1–9 echo the teachings of the Shema (Deut 6:4–6):

> "Hear, O Israel: The Lord our God, the Lord is one. You shall love the Lord your God with all your heart and with all your soul and with all your might. And these words that I command you today shall be on your heart. You shall teach them diligently to your children, and shall talk of them when you sit in your house, and when you walk by the way, and when you lie down, and when you rise. You shall bind them as a sign on your hand, and they shall be as frontlets between your eyes. You shall write them on the doorposts of your house and on your gates." (ESV)

A few verses later in Deuteronomy 6, the instructions about remembering God's commandments are linked to salvation history and provide another example of the wedding of ideas we find in Psalm 78, namely, that God's people need to remember his laws and decrees and they need to know the saving character of the covenant God who enacted those decrees:

> When your children ask you in time to come, "What is the meaning of the decrees and the statutes and the ordinances that the Lord our God has commanded you?" then you shall say to your children, "We were Pharaoh's slaves in Egypt, but the Lord brought us out of Egypt with a mighty hand. The Lord displayed before our eyes great and awesome signs and wonders against Egypt, against Pharaoh and all his household. He brought us out from there in order to bring us in, to give us the land that he promised on oath to our ancestors. Then the

> Lord commanded us to observe all these stat-
> utes, to fear the Lord our God, for our lasting
> good, so as to keep us alive, as is now the case
> (Deut 6:20–24).

What the lectionary has selected for the reading of Psalm 78 is the introductory call, in verses 1–7, to hear about and know the Lord's praises, mighty acts, wonders, and statutes and then to pass on that knowledge to our children, who will then pass on what they know to their children. The message of this section of the psalm is up-lifting and encouraging. We could use it as the basis for a lesson about the importance of Christian education, cat-echesis, spiritual formation, and evangelism.

However, the tone of the rest of this very long psalm is not upbeat, as it fleshes out what the psalmist meant in saying, "I will utter dark sayings from of old, / things that we have heard and known, / that our ancestors have told us (Ps 78:2–3). Verse 8, which is omitted in the lectionary reading, clarifies that we are to pass on the testimony to the next generation not simply to make sure that they believe and remember and preserve God's commandments but, perhaps more importantly, to ensure that they *learn from the failures of the previous generations that did not remem-ber*, so that future generations of God's people do not be-come like their forefathers and foremothers—"a stubborn and rebellious generation, whose hearts were not loyal to God, whose spirits were not faithful to him" (78:8 NIV).

What follows in the rest of this long psalm is a litany of negative examples drawn from Israel's history that il-luminate the pattern that recurs throughout that history:

- Things go well for God's people;
- They become complacent and forget what God has done for them;

- Their forgetfulness leads to flagrant disregard of God's law and disobedience;
- Disobedience incurs God's anger;
- *But* God's wrath does not have the last word.
- Human misery prompts God to remember
- He again compassionately reaches out in mercy to his people.[3]

The first example on the psalmist's wall of shame is the Ephraimites. The psalmist takes thirty verses to explain how it came about that the sons of Ephraim, who had all the human resources, in terms of skill and weapons, that were necessary for victory, were unexpectedly defeated by their enemies. Simply put, they were defeated because they were disobedient to God, and behind their rebellion and waywardness was forgetfulness. Their mistakes included not keeping God's covenant, refusing to follow God's teachings, failing to remember God's activities, and forgetting all the wonderful things that he had showed them (Ps 78:9–11).

The psalmist's rehearsal of the events of the exodus and wilderness wanderings in verses 9–39 features people's inability to remember, as well as their faithlessness. It also portrays God suffering as the creatures that he has created turn their back on him time and time again. This first recounting of Israel's dark history concludes with the statement that in spite of the people's continuous rebellion and sin, God ultimately "restrained his anger," remembering that humans "were but flesh, / a wind that passes and does not come again" (v. 39).

3. Motyer, *Psalms*, 223.

Verses 40–41 introduce a second accounting of what Alec Motyer calls "the deadly sin of not remembering God's power."[4] The psalmist writes:

> How often they rebelled against him in the wilderness
>> and grieved him in the desert!
> They tested God again and again,
>> and provoked the Holy One of Israel. (vv. 40–41)

And why did this happen? It was because "they did not keep in mind his power, / or the day when he redeemed them from the foe" (v. 42). Israel's forgetfulness has led to God's anger and abandonment. His chosen people are now described as his adversaries whom he has routed and disgraced (v. 66).

But these verses do not mark the end of this dark story. The psalm moves to its climax by reminding us yet again that God did not entirely give up on his rebellious and seemingly unteachable creatures. Although he rejected the tribe of Ephraim, he chose the tribe of Judah, and Mount Zion as the place for his sanctuary, and David as his servant and the shepherd of his people (vv. 67–72).

This grim recital of the history of Israel's amnesia regarding God's mighty acts and his statutes and commandments is "the essential story, the root story from which Israel understands her life in every generation."[5] Parents are to pass this thorough, unabridged account of history on to their children so that their story will be different than that of their forefathers and foremothers. They are to remember both God's great acts of salvation and his commandments, and their lives are to be characterized by obedience, reverence, and covenant faithfulness.

4. Motyer, *Psalms*, 219.

5. Tate, *Psalms 51–100*, 295.

The story rehearsed in Psalm 78 is Israel's story, but it is also our story. We know more of the story than the psalmist does. We know, for example, that God's servant David also failed to remember, and we know that the sanctuary on Mount Zion was destroyed not once but twice. We also know that God's creatures continued to forget him and behave in ways similar to those of their ancestors, exhibiting stubbornness, rebellion, and faithlessness. In other words, humanity's sin problem continued.

This psalm does not end its litany of shame without hope, however. It whispers the gospel as it remembers God's choice of the tribe of Judah and God's servant David, who, of course, points us to David's son Jesus, who will rule forever. The hymnist James Montgomery calls us to hail great David's greater son, Jesus, as the Lord's anointed:

Hail to the Lord's Anointed,
Great David's greater Son!
Hail in the time appointed,
His reign on earth begun!
He comes to break oppression,
To set the captive free;
To take away transgression,
And rule in equity.[6]

So, on this day of remembrance, we are called to remember and pass on a thorough and unabridged account of the story of God to our children, who will then pass it on to their children, who are yet unborn, so that they, too, will place their hope in God, remember his saving acts, and keep his commandments. We are also called afresh to rekindle our love for our compassionate God, whom the

6. James Montgomery, Songs of Zion being Imitations of Psalms, 59.

psalmist names as "the Most High God," our "rock," and our "redeemer" (v. 35).

Scripture: Psalm 78

Questions

1. Why do you think the lectionary includes only verses 1–7 of the psalm and not verse 8, which changes its focus?

2. Do you think we should include the narratives of the failures and disobedience of God's people when we recount the story of God to our children?

3. How was the story of God passed on to you by those who taught you? Was it an abridged version, or did you also hear about the failures and punishments?

4. This psalm reveals God's anger and also his broken heart, his mercy, and his covenant faithfulness. What is your experience of God?

5. This psalm and other passages in Scripture stress the importance of knowing God's mighty acts as well as his commandments. Is this wedding of ideas still important to pass on to the next generation?

6. How does the ending of Psalm 78 anticipate the good news of salvation through Jesus, "great David's greater son"?

Bibliography

Angelico, Fra. *The Forerunners of Christ with Saints and Martyrs.* Inner right predella panel of *Fiesole San Domenico Altarpiece.* Circa 1423 or 1424. Egg tempera on wood, 31.9 × 63.5 cm. Main Collection, the National Gallery, London. https://www. nationalgallery.org.uk/paintings/probably-by-fra-angelico-the- forerunners-of-christ-with-saints-and-martyrs

Augustine, *Confessions.* Translated by R.S. Pine-Coffin. New York: Penguin, 1961.

————. *Exposition on the Book of Psalms.* Grand Rapids, MI: Nicene and Post-Nicene Fathers, Series 1, vol. 8.

————. *The Trinity.* Translated by Edmund Hill Hyde Park. New York: New City, 1991.

Barrett, Charlotte. "Gerard Manley Hopkins." https://writersinspire. org/content/gerard-manley-hopkins

Bede, *A History of the English Church and People.* Translated by Leo Sherley-Price. New York: Penguin, 1955.

Bonhoeffer, Dietrich. *Life Together: The Classic Exploration of Christian Community.* Translated by John W. Doberstein. New York: HarperCollins, 1954.

Bradley, Michael. *Monty Python and the Holy Grail.* DVD. Directed by Terry Gillman and Terry Jones. UK: Python (Monty) Pictures, Michael White Productions, National Film Trustee Company, 1975.

Brueggemann, Walter. *Theology of the Old Testament: Testimony, Dispute, Advocacy.* Minneapolis: Fortress, 2012.

Brueggemann, Walter and William Bellinger. *Psalms.* New Cambridge Biblical Commentary Cambridge: Cambridge University Press, 2014.

Carroll, Lewis. *Alice's Adventures in Wonderland.* Boston: Lee and Shepard, 1869.

"Covid Christmas: High Anxiety around Surging Infections, But Many Won't Commit to Staying Home for the Holidays." Angus Reid Institute, December 7, 2020. https://angusreid.org/covid19-christmas

Davis, Ellen. *Opening Israel's Scriptures.* Oxford: Oxford University Press, 2019.

Farrer, Lauralee. "Babette's Feast—Clips for Discussion." Fuller Studio. https://fullerstudio.fuller.edu/booksbabettes-feast-clips-for-discussion

Herbert, George. "The Bunch of Grapes." Christian Classics Ethereal Library. https://www.ccel.org/h/herbert/temple/BunchGrapes.html

Heuman, Gad and Trevor Burnard, eds. *The Routledge History of Slavery.* New York: Routledge, 2011.

Hopkins, Gerard Manley. *The Poems of Gerald Manley Hopkins.* 4th ed. Edited by W.H. Gardner and N.H. MacKenzie. Oxford: Oxford University Press, 1970.

Jørstad, Mari. "The Life of the World: The Vitality and Personhood of Non-Animal Nature in the Hebrew Bible." PhD diss., Duke University, 2016.

Kidner, Derek. *Psalms 73–50.* Downer's Grove, IL: InterVarsity, 2014.

Luther, Martin and Helmut T. Lehmann. *Luther's Works.* Edited by Jaroslav Jan Pelikan and Helmut T. Lehmann. Saint Louis, MO: Concordia Publishing House, 1958.

Mi Yodeya. "Why do people stand for Psalm 100?" https://judaism.stackexchange.com/questions/44357/why-do-people-stand-for-psalm-100

Motyer, Alec. *Psalms, By the Day: A Working Translation with Analysis and Explanatory Notes, and a "Pause for Thought" Based on the Passage Read.* Fearn, Ross-shire, UK: Christian Focus, 2016.

Reno, Russell. *In the Ruins of the Church: Sustaining Faith in a Diminished Age.* Grand Rapids: Brazos, 2002.

Rodriguez, Junius P., ed. *The Historical Encyclopedia of World Slavery.* 2 vols. Santa Barbara, CA: ABC-CLIO, 1997.

Sunukjian, Don. "Four Things Can Happen When You Alliterate, and Four of Them Are Bad." Preaching.com. https://www.preaching.com/articles/four-things-can-happen-when-you-alliterate-and-four-of-them-are-bad

Tate, Marvin E. *Psalms 51–100.* Nashville: Thomas Nelson, 2003.

Vayikra Rabbah 9:7, https://www.sefaria.org/Vayikra_Rabbah.9.8?lang=bi&with=all&lang2=en.

Vaux, Sara Anson. "Letters on Better Movies." In *Reframing Theology and Film: New Focus for an Emerging Discipline,* edited by Robert K. Johnston, 88–108. Grand Rapids: Baker, 2007.

Woolf, Jenny. *The Mystery of Lewis Carroll: Discovering the Whimsical, Thoughtful and Sometimes Lonely Man Who Created "Alice in Wonderland."* New York: St. Martin's, 2010.